Love Th

& Eliminate The Pain

The Business Manager's
Operating Manual

for Selecting & Implementing an ERP System

Archway Publishing books may be ordered through booksellers or by contacting:

Archway Publishing
1663 Liberty Drive
Bloomington, IN 47403
www.archwaypublishing.com
1-(888)-242-5904

ISBN: 978-1-4808-0618-4 (sc)
ISBN: 978-1-4808-0619-1 (e)

Library of Congress Control Number: 2014903614

Printed in the United States of America

Archway Publishing rev. date: 04/30/2014

Contents

Why You Need This Book 1

   What is ERP? 1

   Where Does It Hurt? 6

   Taking the Cure 8

Part I: Know Your Enemy - Identifying Symptoms 16

   Millstones Around Your Neck 19

      Millstone 1: Ignore, Repair, or Replace 19

      Millstone 2: Legacy Systems 24

      Millstone 3: What to Measure 25

      Millstone 4: Intelligent Numbers 29

      Millstone 5: We've always done it that way! 32

      Millstone 6: Common Sense 34

      Millstone 7: False Valuation 37

      Breaking Free 38

   One by One 40

   To Catch a Thief 47

   Working Smarter 55

   Chaos Happens 61

   You Want It When? 66

      Fear of Loss 66

      Can We Take the Order? 70

   Left Behind 76

   Explosive Growth 80

Part II: Divide and Conquer - Finding the Cures............................85

  Right Thing, Right Place, Right Time..............................91

  Simplify..100

    Forces..105

    Elements..106

    Templates and Reality...115

  Strive for Normal...119

  OOP not Oops..146

  Keep It Clean...152

  See the Forest And the Trees...158

  Order Pizza..173

  DIY..179

  One Brick at a Time..188

  Putting It All Together..194

Rewards of a Healthy Database...208

Index..210

Why You Need This Book

Remember when things came with an operating manual that actually answered most of the owner's questions? Some products may still come equipped with such a guide, but that is certainly not the case for selection and implementation of company-wide, management information systems, or enterprise resource planning (ERP).

When documentation is available, it may not be very helpful.

Enter the person's last name in the *Last Name* field...

A primary feature of this book is guidance on the subject of identifying specific needs in the first place and then distinguishing — based on value — between the available solutions. All of these issues are best addressed by a process of simplification, clarifying and separating the fundamental issues relative to their levels of importance.

This book is for the thousands of business managers who are faced with the pressing need to improve their company's information systems; whether by a major course correction to existing systems, or by starting completely from scratch.

What is ERP?

Talk to any number of software vendors and the definitions you get will vary all over the map. In fact, the acronym in my view is entirely misleading, because it starts with the results at the highest level. But as we will reveal, these types of integrated systems are built from the ground up, not the top down. Therefore from my perspective, the purpose of an ERP system is collect and manage the data generated by all the business activities throughout an entire business (enterprise). Higher level functionality (managing resources and planning activities) can easily be added, but the primary objective is connecting everything, utilizing a single database system, providing the foundation for everything else you will want to do with that information.

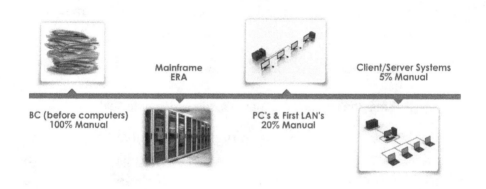

ERP has evolved along with the supporting computer hardware technologies. As the time-line above suggests, the ability to connect many diverse processes, has been partly a function of the hardware available. Before computers (BC), everything was recorded on paper, making connections impossible. In and out baskets were the only connecting tool, and that led to excessive copying and lags at every stage.

Next came mainframes, which are costly and only within the reach of large companies. When those computers first arrived, they mostly handled order processing, purchasing, accounting, etc. Other specialized tasks such as engineering, were still activities requiring manual entry of results into systems for purchasing and scheduling.

When PC's and networking arrived, we started to see special purpose application software become available, such as, computer aided design (CAD), but those applications remained disconnected from the other data management systems. Even in this era, manual entry and reentry of information was (and still is) typical, leading to the term *"islands of information."*

Only recently have systems evolved that now offer true connectivity across the entire organization. With a centralized database, contained in a modern SQL structure, we now have the best of all worlds. The ERP foundation provides the unified data structures to support an uninterrupted flow of information and connectivity to the special purpose applications each business needs. It can be the plumbing system, connecting everything.

Because these concepts are still relatively new to many business managers, and also because there are so many different ideas on how to even define such a system, the process of selecting and implementing ERP is complicated and risky. The choices are vast and the guidance for making the important decisions will often add to the confusion rather than clarify.

Based on typical results for ERP implementations, managers could use some help with this very common problem. This starts with determining the right questions to ask in the first place, and then decision makers need real answers that will prepare them for the important work ahead.

Management will also require a clear benchmark, a sober assessment of the current processes, to establish the standards by which they will measure their level of achievement. Start with a stake in the ground from which all progress will be measured. How else should you quantify your success?

3

Just getting a system up and running does not constitute success, because from that point the real work only begins. At that stage you have reached the first "*Go Live*" milestone where management expects to see the results, in terms of measureable improvements over prior processes.

Methods that sort through, prioritize, and quantify the primary objectives and the key measurements of success are a major topic. This work can only begin once you establish standards for the kinds of information and how it is described, which is actually needed to attain your company's objectives; collecting useless information is a serious waste. To measure things you first have to decide how to identify what you are counting, and the units of measure that make sense in each case. While this may sound trivial, knowing what to measure and how to value each item's qualities, is critical to collecting meaningful information.

Since there are many kinds of businesses, each with specialized needs, this book has a focus on the specific needs of companies that are involved with manufacturing and selling products, as make-to-order manufacturers. However, the general principles apply across many types of businesses. All businesses rely on accurate and timely information, as they seek to measure and manage their company's activities, for optimum productivity.

The exact details and structure of information will be different from one company to another, but there are many principles for its organization and management that are elemental. These principles are relatively easy to understand when explained in non-technical terms; a key goal of this book. We start the how-to part from a basic level, so every reader will see the progression from simple building blocks of data, to complex and powerful structures that reflect the value and true character of your products.

In any business that is managed using methods involving constant process improvement, technology decisions affecting the entire organization may sometimes need to be made, to address new demands on information systems. Changing accounting software, new engineering systems, or especially something as vast as an ERP system, is also life-changing throughout most of your organization and can threaten disruption and instability.

However, as frightening as these prospects may be, they can also present attractive opportunities. We will explore the many benefits that accrue from making this kind of investment, and how to achieve your objectives with the lowest cost and least frustration.

These kinds of changes are not about small improvements. As Michael Hammer pointed out in his ground-breaking book *Re-engineering the Corporation*, minor tweaking (5-10% improvements) of business processes is simply continuous improvement, but large gains are only achieved through a complete re-engineering of major processes. At the center of those profound improvements, you will always find data that has been collected and used to support the decisions and then measure and control all the processes throughout every facet the business. No well managed company runs without excellent management information.

These profound changes are in fact opportunities to start with a clean sheet of paper, and build the leanest processes, applying current technologies to support the quest for optimum productivity. We will pay particular attention to simplification methods used at all levels, from the initial sorting out of information, to the organization of processes for speed and accuracy.

Information systems represent substantial investments, in financial terms as well as commitments for time from the top down. The driving force behind such costly change is usually the result of great pain that has been inflicted by the many shortcomings of the current "legacy" systems that your company employs. Or it could also be due to the lack of features and capabilities that are urgently needed, but which are missing from the currently outdated systems. One goes hand-in-hand with the other, and the solution is a fresh start.

Keeping ahead of the pack in almost any manufacturing industry, requires top-notch tools of every kind, including the information system that connects everything. These are complex and difficult choices, often getting into technical territory that is unfamiliar to most business managers other than IT experts. So of course business managers often lean on expert advice. And therein lies the rub!

Advice on any topic will likely be colored by the advisor. It is human nature, people will put their own spin on things, even when they have no awareness that they are doing so. To reduce the impact of this effect, decision-makers must do their own homework and learn the big-picture concepts themselves — at minimum. And now you have the operating manual you need to get started.

Where Does It Hurt?

When something goes wrong with your body, the problem often makes itself known in the form of pain; through messages instantly sent to your brain, raising an alarm, quantifying the intensity, and identifying the source of the problem. Businesses are not born with such complete, accurate, all-encompassing neural networks, but it is possible to create a similar system.

Some pain is indicative of minor irritations, while other pain might signal a serious ailment requiring immediate attention. The triage of sorting out the important warnings from the noise of many other less critical problems, is necessary to conserve precious resources and ensure time is not wasted on non-essential work. Like the problem of diagnosing illness in a patient, collecting all the necessary metrics and prioritizing their importance is prerequisite to prescribing the best course of treatment for improving the health of a business.

All of those critical measurements of health are contained in the data a business routinely collects, but there can be a large difference between simply handling information, and managing it in a useful manner.

Information scattered among multiple systems, disconnected and difficult to view from any meaningful perspective, is of little value. The cure is organization of your data, into well-designed structures, which allow fast and easy access to all of that valuable information, presented in views that support good decision making. Information systems can also function as the plumbing that connects all of the many processes taking place throughout your organization. Understanding and optimizing these connections, has a profound impact on overall throughput.

This may sound simple, and there are a thousand software developers ready to sell the perfect solution. There are also plenty of options for hardware to collect, store, and present your data. There are even solutions providers to help install, configure, train, and even input data. There is no shortage of bricks and mortar.

However, your problem is not just one of identifying the most urgent pain. Nor is it simply a matter of choosing the right cure. After those decisions have been made, then comes the real challenge of following through with all the chosen therapies until the pain is gone. Following the regimen takes courage and commitment, but the results will be well worth the effort.

We will put special emphasis on symptoms, through examples of real world problems. Learning to indentify the core problems, is key to successful re-engineering. Sorting out the real indicators of illness from the large volume of the measurements is the goal. These warning signs are often going off in many places simultaneously, but there are methods of sorting, organizing, and presenting this information for analysis and decision making.

Once all the symptoms are clearly identified, we need to move quickly to prescribe an appropriate cure. In this stage, all the previous good work of identifying and quantifying the issues will make the diagnosis that much clearer. Later chapters will present methods for putting all of this into the context of your overall business processes, identifying where and how to collect exactly the right the data that your business needs, with the minimum of cost and intrusion into the processes being measured. This is a large order to fill, but well within reach with the correct approach.

Taking the Cure

Pressure to alleviate the pain from these symptoms, may increase from time-to-time, but it is also very common for companies to procrastinate taking their prescribed cure; "...saw the doctor and got the prescription filled, but haven't started taking it yet."

Some of that procrastination may be the result of well founded fear of the many risks ahead, a large number of which will be completely unknown at the beginning of the process. What is known is that these types of projects are inherently over budget, take far longer, and often require bruising compromise to produce results. Statistically 35% of ERP systems implementations fail.

Fortunately those failures do not represent the only possible outcome. With the right approach to designing and implementing your plan and the management commitment to following through with the cure, the pain can be alleviated at reasonable cost, on time, and with rapid return on investment.

The timing for implementation and the selection of technology can be a double-edged sword. Hesitation in implementing important and useful technology can leave your company at a disadvantage. Yet careless selection or hasty implementation can waste resources and further delay the results your company so desperately needs. Vendors often do little to help, and frequently benefit from making the choices appear more technically complicated than necessary.

Here again we discuss the importance of learning and understanding your specifications, and evaluating those requirements in terms that make sense for your business; not just a standard shopping list of features and functions. You will need tools that provide measureable improvements, not simply software upgrades.

One point most managers will agree on is; if you cannot measure activities in terms of results, it is hard to improve anything, much less be sure of what to fix.

For example, what sense would it make to establish a highly detailed budget and then operate without the means to record and categorize expenses? In a similar manner any activities taking place in your business, should have measurable costs and output. However, without the ability to collect and present the necessary data, management decisions will be subjective. These kinds of measurements are critical tools for process improvements.

Well designed and implemented information systems provide the perfect platform for collecting and presenting these metrics — economically and with the lowest impact on the activities being measured. This important point will be discussed in some detail, since every measurement activity has associated costs and will intrude into the process being measured. We want to find ways to collect our measurements that fit into the process, rather than interrupt the very activities we are trying to optimize.

Among the many other impediments to success, in fact one of the most difficult issues, will be the internal resistance and disagreements, from your management team and workers. As with most important decisions, a key ingredient to success is "buy-in" from the people that will be involved in the implementation process.

Most managers know that without buy-in, even your most carefully made plans will be starting out with serious handicaps, and the risk of complete implementation failure is much higher. Building consensus and support within your management team is critical, and the best way to achieve those goals is with solid and convincing information. Here again, it is mandatory for everyone to do their homework. There is no "opt-out" from this process, no delegation of the responsibility will suffice; every key player needs to learn the relevant facts, in order to make good decisions.

The young minds in your organization are great at absorbing new ideas and embracing cutting-edge technologies, but often lack the experience to put those concepts to the best use solving problems. These highly talented people will perform key roles, however; beware of the strong influence they feel from the latest technology trends, many of which will be abandoned as the market decides winners and losers.

In general, be very careful when selecting technology based on "it's the latest", because much of that will turn out to be bleeding edge or flash-in-the-pan fads. More experienced managers may understand their business problems with much greater clarity and perspective, yet may not be up to speed on the new technologies available to address them. This component of your team will have a lot to contribute on the requirements and measurements side of the equation, but they will need help understanding how the latest technologies can be applied to address those problems.

Here we will attempt to find a common ground, where once the tasks are clearly mapped out, the strengths of each participant can be utilized,. Finding that sweet spot is much more likely when everyone fully understands the true nature of the problems and solutions under consideration. Another goal of this book is to help explain many key concepts, using real world examples, with messages that are relevant to manufacturing businesses of all kinds.

This book is full of examples of very common problems in real manufacturing businesses, with careful explanation of the causes and how the solutions were successfully applied. If your team needs some convincing to pull in the same direction, logic always works better than brute force or commands. These case-studies and the solutions they employ are meant to reveal the problems and distill down the complexity of many issues, so that everyone on your team can envision how these solutions can be applied to your company's painful problems.

Once you have completed the work of achieving buy-in, you can enjoy the added benefits, where all the parties:

- feel their needs and interests have been appropriately addressed,

- fully comprehend how the new tools and approaches can help solve their problems,

- and are now prepared to support the process with enthusiasm and creativity.

In most companies, it is the most experienced management that decides which investments will be made and how the money will be spent. They are the ones who "hold the purse strings", so important changes do not happen without their approval, if not their insistence. Precious resources of time and capital, particularly in today's tight economic conditions, should be very wisely invested, but failure to react to change, with appropriate improvements can be just as risky.

For the financial decision-makers we need strong ROI projections, based on comparisons between current and future methods and costs. This comparative perspective—from current to projected values—

should prevail across the all of your business process assessments. The true return on this type of investment should be measured in terms of major gains in the overall throughput of the organization — productivity. We are not measuring small improvements in narrowly defined processes; we intend to see large gains due the synergistic effects of connecting all the business processes for faster and more efficient flow of information.

All of this preparatory work is further complicated by the fact that, most of the input decision-makers will receive from associates, experts, vendors, consultants, etc., *will complicate the decision process, rather than simplify it.* Advisors will usually have a vested interest in a particular outcome, which may include maintaining the status quo. As details are acquired about potential solutions, it may seem impossible to choose, and those details can also make it more difficult to comprehend the real issues at hand. The entire process can easily get bogged down with apparently conflicting facts from the many advisors.

The key to correctly making these critical decisions is the ability to get out of the weeds and simplify your view of the situation. Clear understanding of the underlying sources of your problems is half of the solution, and you need to know how to identify them.

The objective of this book is to provide a few guidelines for simplifying these decisions by distilling complex issues into a small number of clear, basic elements... empirical knowledge. Acquiring that knowledge requires sorting through the information available, distinguishing between relevant details and the many distractions raised as part of the process.

To meet this objective, one approach is to use case studies from the author's manufacturing management experience; War Stories is the common term, and those actual experiences are told to make specific points. Each relates to one or more of the common maladies that businesses acquire, and which often become more debilitating as the company grows.

This volume is relatively short, and purposefully non-technical; in a word — simple. It only seemed right, since the core concept is simplification, that complicated explanations and highly technical language should be avoided at all cost.

Part I: Know Your Enemy - Identifying Symptoms, provides a number of typical examples illustrating real-world painful problems and the solutions applied in each case. This is the war story part of the book, where some of the most common examples of waste and disorganization are recognized and corrected, utilizing principles of simplification and sound data management.

Also this part begins with a large chapter with many sub topics, devoted to those ideas that hold back improvement, i.e. millstones around your neck. This is a collection of some of the most common reasons people avoid change.

Then the chapters in Part II: Divide and Conquer - Finding the Cures, illustrate the key concepts providing the basic toolset and techniques, that apply toward finding your own cures and building them into your own implementation process. These are the core concepts addressing how such problems can be simplified and viewed in the context of normal business processes, resulting in breakthrough improvements on multiple fronts.

There is a strong synergistic effect from viewing information systems from this perspective. Once a solid foundation is laid based on these principles, future improvement gains require progressively smaller investments, in terms of both money and precious time.

Synergy: Where the whole of a system is greater than the sum of its parts. (Wikipedia)

This accelerating return on investment happens because, from a synergistic perspective;

1 + 1 can equal 3 or more

While this statement makes no sense in terms basic arithmetic, in process flow it is commonplace for shared resources to benefit two or more processes; one cost, two benefits. With a consistent focus from such a synergistic perspective, as your business gets its data well organized and working efficiently, every process also becomes easier to manage for maximum profit.

Buckminster Fuller was an architect of great renowned for his Geodesic dome and other architectural and design creations. He was also an inventor with many patents to his name, and he wrote several very unusual books. One of the strangest was; *Operating Manual for Spaceship Earth*, first published in 1968. This book put forth a number of stimulating ideas, including my reference to this book as an operating manual. However, for me the most thought provoking ideas were the Fuller's concepts of synergy and the synergistic man.

Fuller made synergy a term that became widely used, but the idea of the synergistic man which is often overlooked, was even more profound. By synergistic man he described a type of person who was widely aware of the world around him, having sufficient knowledge to be as self-reliant as possible, while still living in a technologically changing environment. This was difficult from Fuller's early twentieth century perspective, and probably much more today, but the goal remains very worthwhile.

A practical example; while you may not be able to rebuild your own transmission, you should know enough about it to avoid being taken advantage of by your mechanic. It is not always necessary to know all of the details, in order to make a correct value judgment.

Appling this concept to the problems associated with selection and implementation of information systems, as decision-makers we must know enough about a lot of things to ensure the best outcomes.

In the world of data, software, and hardware, it is unavoidable that some level of knowledge is necessary in order to make good decisions. The following chapters are an attempt to focus the effort on those key concepts that really matter, leaving out details less critical for our purpose.

When we take away the hype and technical jargon applied to ERP systems, in the end we are simply buying, and then putting to use, a set of tools.

Part I: Know Your Enemy - Identifying Symptoms

It is interesting how difficult it can be to identify the true problem, especially in a complex situation, but even in apparently simple situations. This is an issue that is so well known that we have common expressions such as; "... *can't see the forest for the trees*." How often do we view our own problems from an over-complicated perspective? Do we tend to obfuscate the issues, rather than getting right to the true source of a problem?

I had a friend in furniture manufacturing, who was (and still is) quite successful, but in need of improvements related to the quality and output volume from his production methods. The plant was setup with a very traditional workflow for this type of product, where lots of components and subassemblies were joined together as the product progressed down an assembly line.

We were standing in his final inspection area, looking at a logjam of products held up for "touch up", which meant minor repairs to the fit and finish. He was using much the same methods for repair that most others in the industry were using, but was hoping I might know of some new technology that would allow this work to be completed in less time.

He asked me; "What can we do to get this process flowing at a faster rate?"

I replied that he should not focus on any of the activities in the touch up area, but instead turn around and look back down his production line. "Every defect you are touching up was created down there somewhere. Let's find the sources of these problems and eliminate the need for all this tedious and wasteful repair work.", was my suggestion.

He immediately admitted that this observation was correct, but almost as quickly forgot about the whole conversation and let the assembly process continue as it was. His response was in part because he perceived the difficulty, in pinning down and correcting the many problem sources, was too great in his large complex factory. So he went back to looking for better touch up materials.

If you cannot even identify the true sources of your problems, or worse, you can see them but fail to act, there is no way you will succeed in overcoming them. There can also be many encumbrances, making it difficult to clearly see the problems in first place, or to put the correct value on issues.

The first chapter in this section is about those encumbrances; millstones weighting you down and restraining your ability to move freely and see things from a useful perspective.

The key to making excellent decisions, is in collecting the appropriate measurements, monitoring throughput of the processes, and building excellent tools to view that information from the best perspectives. This critical data and its proper presentation, enables your team to see the bottlenecks and inefficiencies throughout your business processes, and then respond appropriately.

It is fundamental to recognize the kinds of information that will provide a true and accurate picture of health and productivity of your company. Just as important is how your processes are quantified and measured, which is also a key to how data should be organized in the supporting structures.

It is particularly important to collect your data using methods that cause the least possible interference with the activities you wish to measure. Finally, once good data has been collected, the last step is putting the information in front of the people who can use it to make improvements. The organization and presentation of that information can have a large effect on the outcomes, therefore flexibility in presentation views is extremely useful. These activities we monitor are the processes by which quality and productivity are measured, and the results form the basis for change.

To collect good data at reasonable cost, requires careful planning, and a ground up strategy for implementation. The first part of this book will provide a wide range of reasons, while the second part offers the methods.

- Organize the data you collect

- Care for it; keep it clean and safe

- Then you will have the foundation for whatever you want to build

Millstones Around Your Neck

Everyone from time to time suffers from baggage they carry, in the form of "truths" and assumptions that guide their decisions. Here we examine some of those millstones that constrain our thinking and result in repetition of mistakes, even when that thinking has been proven to be incorrect.

These millstone examples are numbered and listed in that order, but that sequencing is not intended to indicate any priority and level of importance. Nor are these few examples of millstones meant to be a complete list of these kinds of wasteful encumbrances, holding managers back from making the best choices for their companies. These few selections are only meant as a sampling to inspire awareness of the pitfalls from these kinds of assumptions.

Millstone 1: Ignore, Repair, or Replace

One of the worst of these millstones is represented by the appalling adage; *"If it ain't broke, don't fix it."*

This concept is so deeply imbedded in our thinking, that continuous improvement coaches have developed the counterpoint to it; *"If it ain't broke, break it!"*

Translating this millstone into a business example; "The bearings on one of our machines are really getting noisy, but the workload is heavy, so we need to avoid down time. Let's just keep a close eye on the lubrication and hope for the best."

What the machine operator knows of course is, the cost of replacing the bearings on a routine basis (before failure) would be reasonable and could be scheduled for a slow time in the workload for that machine. Whereas, waiting until the repair becomes urgent, could mean replacement under the worst conditions, right in the middle of a job. This is short term thinking at best, and results in higher operating costs over the longer term.

Never the less, choices involving putting off maintenance are made routinely, by well-meaning managers. Weighing in favor of their decisions to delay, we have the frugality of the short-term, cash management perspective. It can sometimes be just as bad to fix the problem with a huge single repair, that fails to improve the overall output of the process and just maintains the status quo. Many of these poor decisions or non-decisions, are caused by failure to correctly identify the real issues, which of course leads to costly mistakes.

As Eli Goldratt pointed out so well in his thought-provoking business novel *The Goal*, cost accounting can completely distort the true picture, even when the metrics collected are correct values.

This seemingly illogical statement is valid, because cost accounting is designed to present cost data from a particular perspective; usually short term and focused on certain measurable, incremental aspects of the overall process. These measurements, while they look very accurate and reliable, can be deceptive and may result in seriously wrong decisions.

In Goldratt's novel, one very expensive, newly purchased machine was the immediate focus of attention, and that machine got all the resources directed toward it, which of course distorted the results from normal conditions. The effect of focusing on the new machine rippled through the entire operation. As resources were diverted to the new machine, so were they denied other work centers, skewing the results even further.

By the measurements that the cost accounting presented, the machine investment was deemed to have a strong ROI, because it was producing more parts per hour than the previous methods. However, at the same time, the entire plant was still frightfully inefficient, with no improvement at all in overall throughput. As dumb as that sounds, assessments like that happen all the time, particularly when managers are defending the investments they supported.

It is also important to bear in mind that years of avoided preventive maintenance are not overcome simply with the purchase of a new machine. Nor is the overall productivity likely to rise when nothing has been done that improves the overall work flow. That type of narrowly focused, short sighted thinking also leads to a lax attitude by the workers. It becomes obvious that management has little sincere interest in either maintenance much less improvements so, why not just let things go until they fall apart?

Ongoing care for every asset is just good management. That logic is also a core concept for continuous improvement processes. How can we be improving if we cannot even maintain the value of our current investments?

From one accounting perspective (asset valuation), if we only reinvest in new assets equivalent to the amounts that we claim for depreciation, we will simply be maintaining the status quo in financial terms.

Most factory managers understand the importance of preventive maintenance, with regard to machinery and buildings. At a financial level, managers often understand that equipment reaches a point where replacement makes more sense than constant repair. This may be due to rising cost of maintenance, or because the asset has become obsolete due to the introduction of new features or improved technology.

It is relatively simple to calculate the return on investment, replacing worn machinery, especially when quality and output are also of concern. It is easy to see the value of investing in newer equipment when quality and quantity of production will increase, while maintenance costs are reduced. However, software is frequently viewed much differently, and it often seems much more difficult to calculate the returns, or even measure productivity at all.

There are lots of compelling reasons to ignore the need to improve software systems, but none of these stand up to serious evaluation if we consider the larger picture. Later chapters in this book will reveal methods to put into perspective all of the true factors that should be considered.

One of the largest advantages that software systems can provide is integration of processes. Single-purpose applications can become islands of information that lack connections to the other related activities. In many cases, such applications are necessary because they are the best solution for a specific need; however, it is very important to also consider methods that connect those applications to the other components in the process.

For example, you may need a particular engineering software due to its unique capabilities for your industry application. The solution becomes much better when you can connect that engineering tool to your material database, and also the output from engineering directly to the production tools that will aid in their manufacture.

The earliest design and engineering tools were mostly islands. They were great for drafting lines and arcs, but were disconnected from the materials, machines, and processing activities needed for manufacturing. With a disconnected island such as that, the engineer produces only a dumb drawing, with no other information contained in the design, leaving many additional steps before the full manufacturing picture is completed.

The more integrated approach utilizes engineering software in conjunction with an ERP database that allows users to specify each material as the design progresses, creating a bill of materials (BOM) as the design progresses. And even better tools allow engineers to apply the cutting, boring, shaping and operations, based on the specific capabilities of the equipment that will do the processing.

Those kinds of engineering tools can even integrate processes for the generation of machine instructions for computer numeric controls (CNC), combining multiple engineering steps into one interface.

A very large benefit from this kind of integration is due to fact that the user completes all related tasks at one sitting, rather than having to revisit the design. For example, if only the drawing is completed by one individual, and then the BOM and other work is done later, either by the same person, or worse, by someone else then each step requires the operator to familiarize himself all over again with the design. Alternatively, if the user has integrated engineering software, all of the steps are completed at the same time, eliminating the need to study and relearn all the project details in order to accomplish subsequent procedures.

Such integration is a special and potentially powerful attribute that the most modern software systems offer. With these fully connected systems, we can view the entire workflow and relate multiple sources of vital information, relying on the underlying data structures as the plumbing, rather than manually re-entering information required by the disconnected activities.

With an appropriate view of the overall processes at work in your company, the reasons and timing for improving any of your investments will be much easier to visualize; whether the investment is in machinery, materials, manpower, or the software that connects your flow of information.

It is never a good idea to wait until something brakes before taking steps to replace it. In fact, lean companies continually re-evaluate every aspect of their businesses, always looking for things to improve.

Millstone 2: Legacy Systems

While the first millstone touched on the problem of disconnected or out of date islands, this millstone is important enough to merit its own category. Here we are talking about systems that were originally implemented as the end-all integration, but for various reasons they are now out of date and lacking important functionality. These large millstones can be intractable and are very difficult to replace.

Legacy systems tend to fall into one of two general categories:

- *Purchased systems*, built or installed by parties outside the company, which could be either name brand software, or something built to specifications for the company, or a combination of both

- *Home grown,* either built from scratch internally, or stitched together applications, connected to databases

Your legacy system could fall into either one of these, and comprise a major millstone. Symptoms for this millstone are abundant and easy to spot. Here are a few examples:

- Difficult or impossible to connect your database to other systems

- Your software has not been upgraded in years, and is becoming incompatible with newer hardware

- State-of-the-art features are not available, putting your business at a competitive disadvantage

- Customizations are very costly, painfully slow to bring to completion, and often over budget due to unexpected problems

- Even reports or user-interface changes are a pain

- Errors happen a lot, but may difficult to identify

These are just a few major categories of encumbrances and waste. Their effects are felt at an accelerating rate, as old or poorly constructed systems age further. The key to finally breaking away from a legacy system is the clear comparison of operating costs, between the current situation and the potential improvements that a new system can offer.

Later chapters provide the means to map out and quantify these differences. It all starts with putting real values on the costs that the legacy system impose on your everyday operations. The true costs of these burdens are difficult to identify and even harder to put a value on, therefore there will be substantial guidance in the following chapters on these important activities.

It is important to note, to a lesser degree, special-purpose software systems can become a legacy millstone, especially if a lot of time and money has been invested. Engineering, quoting systems, and home grown software components, may fall into the legacy category if they are not maintained or lack good connectivity. Some kinds of legacy sub-systems can be connected to a new ERP platform, if the functions provided are necessary and difficult to replace.

We will learn how to get a clearer picture of the effects these old systems and antiquated methods can have and how they impede the very processes they were intended to improve.

Millstone 3: What to Measure

Parts and products produced can easily be counted and measured against precise quality and productivity standards. However the value and impact of an information system is another matter, since the metrics of quality and productivity of non-production activities are less commonly measured.

It has always been a source of amazement, how managers focus on the productivity of shop floor activities to such a high degree, while workers paid several times as much for office work may operate at incredibly inefficient rates, without arousing any concern.

Here is conventional wisdom at work again, resulting in progressively lower productivity over an entire organization. Over my career in management I have found that the clerical and other "office work" can often be a major source of delay. Measuring only the production activities, rather than the entire process, can be a large millstone around your neck, holding back the progress of your business.

Every job that your company pays to have done, should be a direct contribution to the overall goal of making money. Production of your widgets does not happen if someone failed to order the material on time. Every step in the process is either critical or should be eliminated.

Most managers have been educated to believe there are categories, such as; direct labor, indirect labor, clerical work, supervision, management, and so on. These categories make sense from an accounting point of view, but also contribute to a perspective that fails to give sufficient weight to the importance of activities that are not direct labor.

In fact, even those workers categorized as direct, will frequently perform indirect activities (work that does not directly contribute to manufacturing a product). If we step back from the narrow focus of these categorizations, we can see the processes in a much different way, inviting possible throughput improvements.

What follows is a typical example of the limitations these labor categories can impose on our thinking, and how activities traditionally considered indirect, may have huge impact on production flow.

Let us consider, for example, a process where both direct labor and indirect interact. In a large assembly operation, there was a constant problem with shortages of certain components, causing interruptions in the process. When the line has multiple workers, and just one has a shortage that causes the work to stop, that one issue stops all the assemblers on the entire line.

The conventional wisdom may suggest; if the line worker is stopped by a material shortage, he should run and get that material from stock and get back to work. This kind of thinking can be observed repeatedly across many kinds of manufacturing, because it seems to make sense on the surface, however it takes a wider viewpoint to see the problems that will result.

There are many faults with the above solution, not the least of which is the inventory imbalances that will probably result. The assembly worker cares only about getting the production line moving again. His supervisor also thinks that everything is about keeping the line moving, so the matter of inventory recording is minor from his point of view.

However, later when the next project is being setup on the line, and the stockroom is found to be short of inventory, the previous quick fix has become a major show stopper. The whole line may need to be re-configured for something else, simply because a key material is not on the shelf as expected.

In fact, another side effect of this behavior is that residual inventory may be left in the assembly area, often because the workers in their haste had misplaced the items and then failed to return remaining quantities to the stockroom. The very item the line worker rushed to take from stock, often turned up later, under a conveyer or workbench.

The solution to this problem is in a clear definition of responsibility, with the support of the information system to manage the details.

Armed with better planning tools including an MRP system, it becomes possible to schedule material arrivals more accurately. The material requirements for each assembly and the timing of delivery are then much easier to manage. What follows is what would happen on our improved assembly process if a modern information system is in place.

Each assembly batch will be planned and scheduled prior to entering production. A complete package of all materials needed will be pulled from stock by a worker whose sole responsibility is making sure the production keeps flowing with exactly the correct materials. This is called kitting, where the kit is the package of materials needed for a particular batch of products.

Each of these kits is then delivered to the assembly supervisor and put in a staging area, ready for the batch of items on the schedule. The supervisor is required to check the completeness of each package and sign a ticket indicating that all of his material has been delivered as needed. If a shortage occurs, it will usually be due to a bad component or a misplacement of the material on the line. Bad components can be replaced on an emergency basis, with a request from assembly noting the shortage.

Upon proposing this solution at a factory early in my career, all of the line supervisors were in agreement that it would not work, would cause delays, and that I would be looking for a new job within a few weeks.

Instead, my team carefully put our plan into action, checking and rechecking each production batch to ensure the quantities were all correct. Within the following few weeks, where it had been predicted the plan would fail, most supervisors started embracing the system.

First they discovered that the stockroom workers, whose responsibility was for accurate quantities, could count better than the line workers who focused on keeping assembly moving, while being less concerned about correct numbers. In the past, if assembly needed 20, and the carton contained 50, they would take the whole carton and get back to work. Returning 30 later was optional.

Second, by relying on the materials team to deliver the needed packages, the production supervisors were able to focus their full attention on managing the production line throughput and quality.

Third, when the line workers had previously run to the stockroom, they often had little knowledge of how and where things were stored, especially since a lot of the material was special for each project. Therefore the production line workers usually took more time to find what they needed, and of course had less concern about the condition in which they left the balance of the inventory.

As a result of these changes, inventory was much better organized and accessible, since it was managed by a team whose main responsibility was ensuring we had the right materials at all times.

All the same work was being done using the new procedures; it was simply organized differently. When the importance of keeping a clean and well managed inventory was elevated to an equal level relative to "production work", everything worked better, including the production activities.

Millstone 4: Intelligent Numbers

One of my most influential mentors was a software developer named Dave Chopp, who before starting his own company, had worked for Allen Bradley (now also called Rockwell Automation) in Milwaukee, WI. Many people in manufacturing and machinery know that Allen Bradley has been a world leader in electrical equipment of all kinds, including high-tech controls.

What may not be common knowledge today is that Allen Bradley was also at the forefront of material requirements planning (MRP) systems, a need driven by their complex and diverse manufacturing requirements. Dave had been in the software systems department during the development of MRP systems for Allen Bradley, and he shared many of his experiences with me when he acted as a consultant to EBCO, the company I worked for in Sheboygan, WI. Dave was a wealth of knowledge and experience in many aspects of manufacturing planning and control systems, and was incredibly generous advising me on building our system.

One of the gems he shared with us had to do with inventory item numbering schemes; an area of great controversy in many companies even today.

People are often convinced that an item number should impart a great deal of descriptive information to the users of those items. This concept is referred to as "intelligent numbering." The idea is to create a part number (in many cases numbers and letters) that very completely describes the item. Usually the system includes a standard for using components of the item number to represent key features.

Color ↓

Category ⟶ 32-R-157 ⟵ Model

In the above very simple example, the first two digits might represent a collection or category of products, the letter in middle represents the color red, and the final digits are the specific model. Since my first experience with this issue, I have found it to be a contentious topic, especially when setting up new information systems. As logical as this concept may seem at first glance, there are many reasons to avoid intelligent numbering.

First and foremost; it doesn't usually work in the long run. Dave related the experiences he went through as Allen Bradley attempted this approach. Each digit or letter in the scheme was to have a specific meaning. One idea behind this was that with experience, a person familiar with the numbering system could look at any part number and know exactly what it was. In Allen Bradley's case, the total number of products was in the hundreds of thousands, so how anyone could believe intelligent numbering would work seems beyond reason.

Worse, there are never enough characters to fully describe a dynamic and constantly changing line of products. Each time they thought they had sufficient characters to describe their vast line, they came across an option that required one more character. This battle ensued until the numbering scheme had reached 23 characters, when even the diehard adherents to intelligent numbering had to admit it wasn't working. Nor did anyone still believe that the users of the system could ever memorize the meaning of each of those characters.

So after a huge amount of time and effort going in the wrong direction, Allen Bradley threw in the towel on intelligent numbering. In its place, they adopted a much simpler system that still had a little intelligence; the first part of the item number meant a category, such as; motor control, or relay, which limited the memorization to a realistic scope.

Part of the early reasoning behind this notion stems from legacy systems that lacked the ability to quickly retrieve data. But even when I first encountered this issue, computers were sufficiently powerful to allow any label to carry part number and description, as well as many other key identifiers. Why should the part number itself need to describe an item, when the written description is printed right next to it?

This is not to say that naming conventions have no merit; to the contrary, standards are preferred. We are talking about the amount of information that will be conveyed by one data field. Naming, categorization, and other questions about organization and hierarchical structures will always be a major aspect in planning data structures. These concepts about naming and data organization will be covered in detail in a later chapter.

So why would these things be issues when considering a new information system? In the dozens of systems I have been involved with over the years, item numbering, descriptions, and organizing conventions are almost always contentious issues. As a result, in many cases these debates delayed starting the implementation, but this can all be avoided by anticipating these controversies and preparing for them before they become delays.

Almost every company will have two camps; one that sees every reason to number products intelligently, and the other that sees no reason to make it an issue. The second camp understands that the item number is simply a unique key, which the software recognizes, and uses to retrieve all the other descriptive information.

However, when new systems are being implemented, management will always want to carefully review the data before entry, and at that time this argument will inevitably came into play. Depending how strongly the key players feel about this, this argument can delay the implementation process, while agreements are hammered out about how to number materials and products.

Do not let this issue side track your implementation. Consider this issue well before the data entry phase of your project, and be prepared for the potential controversy that may follow.

Millstone 5: We've always done it that way!

Old habits are hard to break. Time after time, during evaluation and implementation of new systems, there will be users who will insist that the new software should behave the way the current legacy system works, or worse, it should mimic the current manual paperwork system.

One of the key points of investing in a new system is to achieve improvements in the integration and processing time for the various tasks. So of course, any new system will include changes in the ways the work is accomplished.

There is one category where keeping things similar looking is sometimes a worthwhile consideration, and that is reports, labels, and documents, particularly those that work well.

For example; documents used by workers become familiar, and changing the format can result in a learning curve and even mistakes. However, if the change is made to improve the readability or add necessary new information to the document, then of course change makes sense. Again, the rule of thumb should be: the change should constitute an improvement in workflow, not just a different look.

Continuous improvement by definition means constant change. As uncomfortable as people may be with that, it is critical to keep an open mind with regard to the refinement of processes. Even strong proponents for improvement in general will sometimes find themselves defending some things partly on the basis of "always done it that way."

On the other side of that coin, there is certainly no reason to change things without good reason. Each component of your system should improve workflow, not simply the appearance of the interface or output. How many software "upgrades" have we all seen, where the only difference is the style of the buttons, or the way a menu is accessed? Cosmetic changes have their place, but we want to focus our attention on better integration and workflow.

Clinging to old ways is probably the most classic millstone of them all. While we are not interested in change for the sake of change, we must also be willing to break old habits when they encumber workflow.

Millstone 6: Common Sense

A popular adage among IT and financial managers during the heyday of big hardware platforms goes:

Nobody ever got fired for buying IBM.

When you think about it, that adage conveys a number of meanings. It clearly implies the wisdom of taking the safe path; don't try anything unproven, go with the well known brand. However at the same time, such wisdom condones mediocrity as a trade off against lesser-known choices.

Also, such safe choices are no guarantee against failure in the overall endeavor. Putting your software on the top hardware platform does not ensure successful implementation. And who has not been burned by the big name brand anyway? That topic would fill another whole book.

The same has been shown with big name software products time and time again as well. The brand name and corporate recognition will not guarantee that all of their customers will be successful.

We have all heard sage advisors confidently proclaim wisdom, such as;

- in this category we always buy from...

- our company isn't big enough for...

- our workers aren't smart enough...

- we need to talk to several references, that are just like us...

Maybe common sense has its place, but not when you are breaking into unfamiliar territory. Of course due diligence is required to vet each candidate supplier and each type of product, but your ERP implementation is unique to your specific needs.

Sherlock Holmes' guiding principle was to carefully collect all the facts, then whatever conclusion they supported will be correct, no matter how improbable it may seem. The other characters surrounding Sherlock, were solid, conservative, experts, whose common sense always seemed to lead in the wrong direction. Whereas Sherlock would analyze the data, free of common sense, with a completely open mind, which consistently led to the correct conclusion.

We do not even need an example from fiction to prove how misleading common sense can be. Here for example is a learning experience from my life as a high school sophomore, excited by math and science, of all things.

That was a milestone year for me, changing my outlook on the use of logic to solve problems. It was the year I took the first serious course in geometry. Earlier throughout the lower grades, we learned about triangles, and rectangles, and maybe even the Pythagorean theorem, but Mr. Gurney, my geometry teacher, was all about logic and proof. He demonstrated how common sense in most cases was not enough, and in some cases it was completely misleading. A correct answer on one of his tests, was marked as wrong, if it lacked the supporting logical proof.

In fact, our hero at the time, a guy named Euclid who live in Alexandria about 300 BC, was also fooled, as were his followers for centuries later. They all believed in something that seemed so apparent, that it should be provable, but no one could develop a proof that was based on facts, without adding in some common sense (un-provable) terms.

Any carpenter with an ounce of common sense knows that two boards, which measure exactly the same distance apart, at any two locations, will always measure the same distance apart at any point because they are parallel.

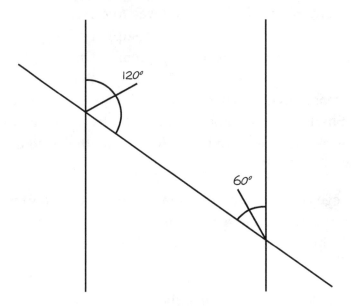

The way Euclid explained it was a bit more abstract, having to do with measuring the interior angles formed by an intersecting line. In the simplest example we have the following graphic. The two vertical lines are intersected by the other angled line. If we measure the angles, and they add up to 180°, then in our plain geometry world the two lines should remain parallel infinitely in both directions.

However, if you went further with your math education, other options were revealed, which are now referred to as non-Euclidian geometry. And it turns out, that the common sense result (the two lines remain parallel, never meeting or getting any further apart), is the only option that is never really true! Why? Because when you back off to see the bigger picture, from space for example, all the parallel lines we draw here on Earth, will meet at opposite poles... always.

Draw a line on your globe of the Earth or just follow the lines of longitude that each intersect the equator at 90°. Follow any two longitude lines up to the North Pole, and what happens? Even though both lines started out perpendicular to the equator, they meet at both poles. Instead of the surface of the Earth, do the experiment in space, and the lines grow farther apart in either direction. Our world is not flat, even though it may appear that way from your current perspective. So much for common sense.

The point of all this is that common sense often works only from a very limited perspective, but when facts are viewed differently, the conclusions might be completely unexpected. This is particularly true when exploring unfamiliar territory. Keeping an open mind, drawing conclusions based on accurate facts and clear logic, beats common sense.

Millstone 7: False Valuation

Although this example has been saved for last, it is by no means the least important. Failure to properly assess the ROI for a large investment can come at great penalty. In addition to the difficulty quantifying unknowns, it is also possible to be encumbered with some common misconceptions regarding the value of an investment.

One misconception is the intrinsic value we put on solid things with physical weight. "He is worth his weight in gold!", "You can feel the value by the weight..." and so on.

Machinery has weight. Software has no weight. Therefore, in some ways, by some perspectives, this lack of physical dimensions may appear to diminish an item's value. Of course such physical dimensions have nothing to do with a software product's ROI potential, but most buyers of intellectual property have at least occasions when this factor has an effect on them.

"We just spent $200K on the machine. Now we have to buy $30K in software to make it productive?"

The machine is one component in the complex web of investments, each taking a piece of your company's capital. ERP software forms an interconnecting communications system, sending the messages that control the processes, which in effect makes it much simpler to measure its effects. It is important to view any investment from an ROI perspective; weighing the investment against the income improvement. It should never be about the salvage value!

What good is your arm without the proper impulses from your brain telling it precisely how and when to move? Software enables the other physical activities, by supplying the right information at the right time. Information systems can coordinate all of the processes and provide feedback for improved productivity, resulting in the same kinds of returned value expected from any other investment.

To arrive at the best value judgment, you need to get over this baggage of setting values based on arbitrary attributes. The investment value should be measured by the difference between expenditures (how much did we spend) and returns (what did we get back). These results are not difficult to measure and calculate.

Breaking Free

The best decisions start with the best specifications. If your needs are poorly defined, you can count on some degree of disappointment. This task must be primarily completed internally, not by outside vendors although their guidance in putting it all together may be be valuable. Assistance with organizing the process is fine, but your company knows its pain the best, so your team must set the primary objectives.

In the end, a pivotal role of such an information system, is in providing the means for measuring overall throughput and costs. That result is the bare minimum return that should be expected, and that is just the starting point.

Do not expect—just because you bought the big brand or purchased from the top consultant—that you are assured success. This is a common misconception that keeps on working for the top names. Success is the product of your commitment and hard work. It cannot be had just by hiring the best contractors or writing the biggest check.

It is human nature to let other influences creep into decisions, but if done fairly and diligently, an ROI approach based on the realistic measurements will always paint the most accurate picture.

Safety in your decisions is ensured by educating yourself to make the best choices. Get the facts, not just the hype or conventional wisdom. There is no common sense solution to a problem of this magnitude that is out of the realm of your experience. There is no silver bullet, there is no Easy Button, nor will an endless amount of money solve your problems.

You must do your homework.

One by One

One of the many apparent contradictions in lean manufacturing is the goal of a lot size of one; meaning nothing should be made in large batches.

Those with much experience in traditional manufacturing, having witnessed the realities of setup time, prep and clean up, material handling, and so on, find it difficult to give up the immediate productivity gains from repetitive processing. These factors make it inconceivable that, when given the opportunity to combine quantities of the same items for processing at certain steps, we would choose to make only one at a time.

One reason that this lean concept is so hard to digest, is that we are accustomed to focusing on only a small part of the entire process. When we step back and see the larger picture, other risks and benefits become apparent. Some of our examples presented in later chapters will demonstrate how easy it can be to let a narrow view of productivity, encumber the overall throughput.

Converse to the lot size of one thinking, we may also encounter situations where even in make-to-order manufacturing, combining at certain steps in the process greatly improves throughput, and even quality. Disconnected, or very manual systems make it difficult or impossible to manage all of the details needed to control and optimize flow under these circumstances. Managing this level of complexity and volume, is more successful when information can be viewed from different angles, to accurately predict the impact of your decisions.

One example of such a situation is from my experience at EBCO, a large laminate furniture maker, manufacturing products for hotels and dormitories, all made to order and in some case completely custom designs. These products were configured to the exact specifications for each project, but many of the options such as colors, were usually selected from a few of the most popular current selections.

The amount of laminate material consumed at this plant was enough that we were a direct account with the manufacturer, bypassing the distributor network, with full truckload deliveries on their trucks. Once in our facility, this material was glued to various cores in our laminating department, which was capable of cutting up and pressing high volumes of these key materials.

Our CEO had instructed me to negotiate with every major vendor to keep our prices as sharp as possible. Since our company purchased in such large volume, I thought my job would be easy.

My first call to our laminate supplier in his New York corporate headquarters office, went something like:

"Hi this is Mick Peters from EBCO, calling to discuss our pricing for the next year."

To which our account manager replied: "Nice to hear from you Mick, what can I do for you today?"

"Well you know our volume is up to X million feet, we were thinking our price should be a few cents lower..."

Interrupting me in mid-sentence, the account manager interjected, almost laughing; "Whoa, you are lucky we are keeping you direct instead of having your purchases go through our Chicago distributor!"

Taken aback I responded; "But we buy a whole truckload a week..."

And again he interrupted with; "Yes but have you ever counted the number of PO's on one of those trucks?

That comment was completely unexpected. I knew the total square footage, and the total dollars we were spending, but I was really not sure how many PO's we cut each week to this vendor.

However, the account manager didn't let me think about that one for long when he answered his own question; "Typical average is 50 PO's per truck... with a typical mix of 80% the same 4 patterns... over and over on separate PO's, which we have to count out and package on pallets. Get the picture? Yes, you buy a lot, but what a pain to process your orders."

Before I could respond to this heavy dose of bitter medicine, he went on; "And how about on your end? Your warehouse guys have to unload and count every pallet by PO, which you probably have to warehouse and then retrieve by each order. But these are the same patterns, so why not just order a bunch of each, and keep them in one place?"

We ended the conversation with his agreement to give me some time to consider his observations.

My lack of important information had put me at a disadvantage, during what started out as a price and terms negotiation. A great deal was at stake for my company, and it was clear that better management of our material requirements was needed.

Like many job shops, our company had relatively manual systems, making it difficult to combine material requirements for purchasing. Also, given the short lead times we had to work with, the moment engineering had each project specified and detailed, purchasing was pressed to get the materials ordered, or risk falling behind schedule. It was a typical fire department.

Another negative we discovered while studying this process, was that we were often purchasing some materials far too early, just to ensure that every material was available when we needed it. Inventory was costly, and of the roughly $1,000,000 of material we kept on hand at any time, a significant percentage was not required in production for several weeks. We were under the false assumption that earlier was better than late, and inventory was our insurance.

Then there was the material storage and retrieval component of the cost equation. Once an order was in the production schedule, the materials had to be retrieved from storage in the warehouse and delivered to the work center where it would be processed. Here it may seem as though the one PO per order approach would be a benefit, but there was a catch.

This is very bulky material, and as flat sheet goods, it lends itself to stacking. In fact, if you do not stack it, the floor space requirements go up exponentially. So we would have multiples of these pallets, each with their specific PO for a production order. And in a typical stack of 10 pallets in a particular warehouse location, where would we find the one we need now? In the middle or bottom of the stack of course.

So now the warehouse worker must un-stack, move temporarily, extract the one they need, then re-stack everything only to repeat the process again for the next production order. The specific material in this example is hard, thin, and very brittle. Winter temperatures in our unheated Sheboygan, Wisconsin warehouse might also drop well below freezing, leading to a great deal of handling damage even before processing started.

Storage racks helped, but keeping track of so many individual pallets (about 50 per week) was a nightmare in itself. Racking reduced the stacking problem, but also added a lot of expense. Since we needed so many, and could not justify the cost or space for numbers of rack spaces we needed. By way of compromise, we still stacked 2 or 3 orders together in each rack space.

Fortunately at that point in time, we were in the process in implementing new computer systems that could allow us to combine material requirements from multiple orders and calculate the total quantities needed for production each week. Functionality like this is called MRP, for material requirements planning.

So then with the capability to combine and time-phase requirements from multiple projects, we could store these materials in large bins for each of the major patterns we used on a repetitive basis. Unloading trucks would be much faster, and with less handling our breakage rates would plummet.

Similar savings would be realized by our vendor as well, since they could now ship total quantities of each pattern together. All the previous sorting into small batches for many individual PO's would be eliminated, along with risk of scratching and breaking.

Armed with this capability, I again called our account manager to explain;

"We took your comments seriously and have invested in systems to allow us to combine and time phase our requirements. We will now place only one master PO per week, with an allowance for a few last-minute specials to be added. If we can guarantee no more than 5 PO's for an entire truckload, what can you do for us in return?"

This time he was the one caught off guard, since he really did not expect that we could do that, especially in such a short period of time.

He replied; "Can you really do that?"

To which I responded; "Yes, because it is in our best interests, we have made the investments to make these changes."

And so he agreed to reduce our price by nearly 10%, due to their substantially lower handling costs, resulting in first year savings to our company of nearly $50,000. This was just in one key material category! We were just getting started.

However, purchasing was only the tip of the iceberg in terms of how we leveraged our information systems in many ways, very often running contrary to conventional wisdom. In fact, this example may not set well with may adherents to JIT concepts, but there is nothing wrong with this approach for material planning, as long as we can still discretely manage the products on our orders. Although the PO quantities were consolidated, we still knew exactly how much of each material was required for each discrete production order.

Prior to our new information system, most data had been on paper. Copies were made for everyone that needed the information, and consolidation of anything was nearly impossible. The amount of paper that had to be processed and filed was a huge burden. As a result, the company increased the number of clerical staff, which actually got in the way and caused even more problems.

This reaction to workload bottlenecks is referred to as "throwing bodies at a problem", which is addressed as a whole topic in a later chapter. It is quite common, especially for small businesses to consider adding staff to address such bottlenecks, after all the work is obviously too much for the current number of people. It seems so logical that if the workload is too much for one person, you will reach a point where you need a second, but also remember, new people will probably need training and time to acclimate to their new position. Their lack of experience may cause more mistakes and delays until they learn.

However in this example, the streamlining of most of our information processing, resulted in fewer staff, who were far more productive, earned higher wages, and were making more profitable decisions.

In this example, we were able to significantly reduce clerical staff throughout purchasing, production control, and shipping. Most people were reassigned to other positions, since the company was also experiencing rapid growth in sales, due to improved lead times for orders.

The key to our solution was first understanding the full impact of the methods and processes we were using. Taking a big-picture view of the situation, we were able to see lots of opportunities for improved workflow and accuracy. Then with a foundational database system, we were able to collect date, view it, and manage the complexity of a high-volume, make-to-order company.

To summarize from the above example, the ability to manage information for business decision making is crucial, not just for efficient day to day operations, but also for decision making and problem solving.

Collect and manage all needed information about your processes in a way that allows for maximum flexibility to view and act on this valuable resource. Manage your data such that your decisions may always be based on the most relevant and meaningful facts.

Empowered with these capabilities, managers can address any kind of business problem, with logical solutions well supported by the best information.

To Catch a Thief

On my very first day as VP of Operations for a popular wooden-case clock manufacturer, I had a meeting with the President and VP of Finance. They both insisted that the company was being robbed at the rate of $10,000 to $20,000 worth of inventory each month!

This was my area of responsibility now, and an effective solution was expected quickly.

The facts of the matter were:

- Inventory balances were completely unreliable

- Monthly physical inventory counts were necessary to determine which items could be put into production

- Key material quantities were repeatedly found to be short of the book inventory

- These problems made it very difficult for this rapidly growing manufacturer to respond to customer orders in a consistent and timely manner

Imagine the full costs associated with this problem. In addition to the monthly write-down of inventory value, there were huge costs of taking the physical inventories, which also interfered with production, resulting in lost sales in many situations.

The VP Finance had hired a detective agency that confirmed one theft, however the actual amount of that was relatively small. The workforce was not particularly large, and although we did not have much security, it was difficult to imagine how such large dollar amounts of such a wide variety of components could find their way out of the building without notice.

At the same time, there was also a dispute with one of our largest suppliers of high-quality brass components. In fact, our company had just returned a pallet full of parts that the quality control department had quarantined as vendor defects. These parts had obvious blemishes, scratches, and tarnishing; all unacceptable for the most visible components in our clocks.

The next day, during a visit to the supplier's manufacturing facility, we found a very well organized plant, with clean work areas, highly trained production workers, and clearly defined quality control standards. Step by step, as we toured the operation, we saw the careful handling of these high-value components, with very few defects generated along the way. Comparing these observations to the large number of components we had recently returned as "vendor defects", it was obvious that something else was at work here.

The vendor was insisting that they were not responsible for the majority of the defects that were found in the returned shipment. Their allegation was that we were causing these defects during receiving, inspection, and especially in production, due to poor handling, when installing their components. However, since they were also keen to maintain a positive relationship and continued sales, they agreed to a compromise settlement, crediting back a portion of the value of the defective shipment.

The first thing we did upon returning to our production facility, was to review the inspection and handling procedures we were using at the time. Incoming inspection of this type of component was thorough, but was not on 100% of the items. They only did sampling, with careful inspection of each lot. Statistically, the quality control department saw no explanation for the total numbers of defects, since the incoming shipments looked very good. We still had no explanation for the damaged components returned regularly from the factory floor, with defects similar to the batch we had sent back.

Although the QC manager was knowledgeable and well trained in the identification of these quality problems, she knew little about how the components were handled in our production process. That was the next stop in our investigation.

Production was all about units per hour and managing costs against the production budget. Each model we were building had a complete bill-of-material (BOM) that listed every item of significant value that was required to produce that finished product. Materials were issued from inventory at the request of the production manager, who was focused on completion of the planned quantities on his production schedule.

Scheduling was critical, since these were consumer products, often scheduled to be delivered for advertized sales events our customers had planned. These were frequently seasonal events, like; father's day, mother's day, Thanksgiving, and Christmas. Failing to deliver on time for our customer's sales events could result in product returns, which may then remain unsold for months, waiting in the finished goods warehouse for the next seasonal sales event.

In the world of our production facility, with the clear priority on throughput and cost management, components were sometimes mishandled in the rush. The assembler was under pressure to build a certain number of units. If along the way a few parts were damaged by rough handling, that could be dealt with later by someone else. Toss the bad part aside and grab another. If we run out at the workstation, get more from inventory.

Bad parts encountered in the production area would be culled out, taken off the production floor, and would end up in the QC department. There they would often be deemed "vendor defects" (meaning the vendor caused them), even though the defects were acquired in our facility, not the manufacturer's. Draw your own moral and ethical conclusions; this was an internal source of unreported waste.

We had uncovered several bad practices and began a program to correct this type of problem, but these issues could not fully explain the inventory losses, although they pointed in the right direction.

All throughout the warehouse and production facility, the processes were organized strictly for low-cost, unimpeded flow from materials to finished goods. The side effects of this seemingly efficient operation were poor control and deferred costs that had to be addressed down the financial road.

After a complete assessment of the QC, warehouse, and production processes, we finally turned our attention to the front office. There we found a bookkeeping department using entirely manual methods.

Everything from engineering data, to purchasing, scheduling, through invoicing, was managed mainly by passing paper documents from one desk to the next. Inventory was maintained on card system similar to a check register, where additions and subtractions were noted and then a new balance was calculated.

The year was 1980 — before PC's — when small to medium manufacturing was just beginning to use computers for accounting, with even less attention to the manufacturing processes.

The inventory system they were using seemed totally logical from an accounting point of view. Accountants call the process back-flushing, and it certainly has its place, but there are situations where it does not work well, particularly where items can be damaged or rejected as defective. That problem had been considered very minor, but that was because there was no way to compare back flushing to actual.

Based on faulty logic this 100% back flush process worked like this: as finished products were completed each day, the accounting department would extend the BOM quantities for each component, and subtract each of those results from the inventory balance.

It seemed so simple... To make one clock it takes:

1 cabinet

1 clock mechanism

1 dial

1 pendulum

etc.

Right?

So it followed (conventional wisdom at the time) that simply back-flushing (subtracting each BOM item from inventory at some time in the production process) would result in a reasonably close inventory balance. Production management was held to a standard cost system by accounting, and there was no particular incentive for anyone to voluntarily report additional costs due to using more than the BOM quantities.

We had already witnessed the process where we caused defects to some parts, then charged them back to the vendor. Although in time, the cost of those actions might be recovered by holding the supplier responsible, these methods resulted in a reduction in inventory quantities, without a corresponding change in available raw material quantities. Management had perceived the detailed accounting for this inventory transaction as an unnecessary and costly step, for which they could adjust the books later.

Then we also discovered another process that was almost off-the-books. This was found in a small department that handled complaints about the products, questions about repair and maintenance, and returns.

Since no one really gave much thought to formalizing any procedures, this department which started very small, took a very pragmatic approach to dealing with the need for occasional spare parts; they would take them from returns, or even raw material inventory, all without any accounting other than an invoice to the customer. Again, the money was managed, but the inventory accounting was not being handled at all.

Shortly after these discoveries, the company installed the first computer system; a main frame type of system with lots of terminals connected to it. While the architecture was impossibly below today's standards, it did provide a very manageable central database, with inventory, sales, and accounting components.

Very little off-the-shelf software was available at the time so we built our own production and inventory management system, basically automating procedures to process each transaction needed to track parts from, receipt to completed finished goods.

Production scheduling triggered pre-issue of high-value materials to a production work cell, under requisitions that could be returned to the production office for data entry. If additional material was needed due to either a discovered or created defect, replacements were easily requested and delivered using a simple manual (like Kanban) system. Each material transaction was then correctly posted for both costs and inventory quantities.

In addition to these material management procedures, we also setup a cycle counting process, which allowed us to get every item balance corrected and under control. Over a short amount of operating time, the cycle counting process revealed fewer and fewer inaccuracies.

Once these systems were in place, we stopped the costly physical inventories that had been a large monthly expense. The new processes were also resulting in fewer production delays due to lack of materials, which gave us confidence that inventory balances were becoming much more accurate.

After several months of operation with the new controls, we approached the end of our fiscal year, and that meant the dreaded and frightfully expensive annual audited inventory. Tags in hand, and with CPA's monitoring the process, we shut down production and hand counted every piece of every stage of every material or product in the facility. Each lot carefully tagged and with part of each tag removed by the auditors for processing.

We knew we were dealing with about $2,000,000 of total inventory, in the various stages throughout the plant. Our last audited inventory revealed tens of thousands of dollars of incorrect values. Since then, our cycle counting had also revealed a large amount of supposedly good inventory, that was in fact defective, all of which had to be written off as it was discovered. Those issues had all been accounted for and current inventory values seem correct.

The audit was the ultimate test of our system's accuracy. Our confidence was high, but the tedious process of counting and then tabulating all of those tags, all under the watchful eyes of the CPA's who knew us to be error prone, weighed heavily on everyone.

When our management team finally met with the auditors, we were sorely disappointed to hear that they were demanding a recount of a large part of the higher value inventory items. The CPA's were highly suspicious that they had been deceived. Maybe the thieves were still among us.

The reason for the suspicion was that the count suggested that after running our business for nearly a year without a physical inventory, on $2,000,000 with over thousands of SKU's, the audit indicated our counts were within $1,500 in total value; less than one tenth of one percent error. The auditors could not believe it, so we recounted with the same result a second time.

We had apprehended the thieves and stopped the losses, all with a very simple set of controls. Even more important than the direct financial impact, a more reliable inventory management system helped improve production throughput, and made our delivery estimates more accurate.

You may read this and conclude; "That would have never happened in the first place at my company, we have much better control..."

Or maybe you are still on the other side of this discussion; "It would not be worth the expense to finitely track all of these details, so we just make occasional adjustments."

As will be shown in later chapters, achieving results such as these does not necessarily have to be complicated or expensive. Managing information well is fundamental to almost any kind of improvement process, and by clearly understanding your objectives, you can do so simply and economically.

Working Smarter

Here we will examine two distinct approaches to bottlenecks constraining productivity:

One option increases the dependency on labor, either by adding staff, scheduling more hours, or just generally working people harder. This approach is based on the short term imperative of avoiding investments that might relieve the pressure.

The second option is to apply technology to increase productivity; whether a machine is needed to increase throughput in the plant, or software and data management systems to help control the processes.

We begin by examining the time honored tradition of adding manual labor. The least effective, but still very popular solution is hiring more people to do the work. Ironically, this is often considered the lowest cost option, because of the low cash flow over the short term.

For some reason, hiring additional workers is often viewed as the least expensive alternative when in fact technology would provide the better return on investment. In the short term this thinking may certainly appear reasonable, since the employee expense is paid out a week at a time. However, the technology based alternative has many advantages over hiring, particularly over the longer term.

Machines and software normally do not vary in terms of the quantity or quality of production output, as long as maintenance is preformed appropriately. Technology solutions are also less likely to need a day off, take a vacation, or just fail to perform as usual because they are having a bad day. Therefore, results are also more predictable, making scheduling more accurate. And the machine or software never demands a raise (upgrade), without an appropriate increase in productivity.

One of the most overlooked negatives to adding staff is that productivity in terms of output per worker hour will actually decrease as the numbers grow. Every manager has seen how adding a second worker requires training, acclimation, and then time for experience to accrue before the new employee gets up to stride. This of course assumes that the employee stays and works out in the position. Keep increasing the size of the team, and those effects multiply, dragging down the overall throughput.

And then as those numbers grow, you will eventually need more supervision, which dramatically increases the overhead component for the group. The larger the work force, the more difficult it becomes to evaluate individual performance as well.

Another common tactic along these same lines is to increase the working hours for the existing employees, which may be better than hiring, but also has diminishing returns as people tire from the longer work days. At the same time, overtime usually means a higher rate of pay for the work, thereby reducing productivity measured in terms of actual cost per unit of output.

These solutions all have a negative impact on operating costs and productivity. Every effort should be made to find technology solutions to address increased demand. Technology solutions are more predictable, easier to manage, and keep operations in a lean condition. Changes are also easier to make when the team is smaller, with less training and other ramp up costs required.

The worst reason to add staff is pride. Managers are often proud of how many workers they supervise. "There are 100 workers in my department!" While that may sound like a statistic worth boasting about, wouldn't it be better it say; "We manage all of this production with just 10 employees!" Working smarter, not harder is always the better option.

Not just cost of production, but even quality suffers from over staffing. The more people under supervision, the more difficult it becomes to keep quality at the desired levels. There will be newer, less experienced people, having to learn by making mistakes on the job, who will also require more training and guidance from supervisors and management.

Here is an example from a front office situation, where the cost of adding staff was huge. I had just taken a position in a large company that was suffering from a serious overload on almost every department. Purchasing in this make-to-order company was overwhelmed with the sheer volume and variety of materials that had to be ordered on very short lead times. Although the total volume of products was huge, so was the variation in order size and material selections. Failure to deliver our product on time resulted in large penalties for every day late. One reaction by management was to staff up the purchasing department.

In fact, these people were not even functioning as a typical purchasing agent would be expected to work. Tasks such as negotiating prices and terms, were not even attempted, since we were begging for favorable delivery dates. Plus no one had the time to think about anything other than cutting the PO's as fast as possible and getting on to the next order. Our purchasing staff were reduced to the job of typists, as they cranked out orders as fast as possible. Our vendors were for the most part delighted. What seller doesn't love the customer with the rush order, who has no leverage to haggle over prices or terms? Those are the customers that pay the highest prices every time.

In this case a software technology option was ultimately our solution. We had been replacing our manual systems with an integrated database, and had been able to get BOM data input as new orders arrived. For the first time, the company had the ability to manage this precious data in ways never possible on paper. Each order, from one mirror to 500 rooms of furniture, was entered with all the material requirements extended by the quantities. Demand for each material item was assigned dates based on when they would be needed in the production process.

With the ability to calculate total demand for all materials, in the proper time sequence based on when they were actually needed, our purchasing department was able to see the big picture. They could look across combined order demand over time, so that orders for the same materials could be consolidated, saving shipping and handling costs, and reducing the number of PO's to each vendor. A specific example of this was described in the earlier chapter "One by One", where MRP helped cut PO volume and simplify physical handling of the material at the same time.

After complete implementation of the software solution, the departments managing production, inventory, and purchasing were reorganized from scratch. The number of purchasing staff was reduced from three to just one person. During this process, sales increased by about 65% over the prior year, but the integration resulting from the information systems allowed that one person to do a far better job even with the added load of the higher production volume.

No longer were we simply cranking out PO's as fast as possible. Instead, we were leveraging the data tools we had to work with each vendor to improve the flow of materials, resulting in fewer orders, fewer overnight shipments, less begging for unrealistic shipping dates, and a better handle on total volume with each vendor.

One of that company's oldest vendors of a key material had been taking advantage of our chaotic situation for a long time. Once we had the data to understand our trends for their product, we put those materials out for bid to other competitive suppliers. The results were astounding! We discovered that our old reliable vendor was gouging us to the tune of about 10%. Plus the new vendors, anxious for a shot at our business, offered much better terms and more flexible deliveries.

It was a memorable day, when after changing over to the newly selected vendor, I got a call from our CEO, who had the old vendor's salesman in his office.

The call when something like this;

"Mick, I've got Jim in my office and he is fuming over your decision to buy from another supplier! I hope you understand the level of service that this company has provided over the years. Certainly that should be important to us."

To which I responded;

"Yes Bob, I agree that service is important to us, and Jim has always worked with us, but he was given the same specifications as all the other competitors, and even considering his great service in the past, his pricing was way out of line. Why just in one year we will save over $20,000 on exactly the same products."

"Oh and the new vendor has offered a much better delivery schedule, so we will have lower shipping costs and more regular flow of trucks from their facility. However, if you still think we should stick with Jim, it's your company."

Bob was a savvy businessman, and he replied;

"No problem, I'll walk Jim out to his car and let him know he will have another shot at our business next year."

The system we installed to help us manage our information was a large investment for our company — about $100,000 just to get started. However, in just the first year:

- Material purchase price variance (savings over standards) totaled over $50,000

- Inventory was reduced from about $1,000,000 to $600,000, resulting in $400,000 additional operating capital

- Prior to the new system more staff would have been needed, but even with sales soaring, we simply reassigned people to more efficient activities

But the most important benefit was our radically improved productivity, which meant much shorter lead times to our customers. This result was the driving force of our growth, and continued to improve for years after the system implementation.

At that year's Christmas party Bob was boosting; "I have made a lot of investments over the years, mostly in buildings and machines. But that $100,000 I put into this computer system has provided the highest return of anything we have done yet!"

Chaos Happens

This chapter is about forces that compel people to act in opposition to the work flow. We have seen how "throwing bodies at the problem" can be very counterproductive. We have also seen how, even with the best of intentions, people can make decisions that run contrary to the overall goals of their business.

Let us look a bit deeper into how disorganization, the pressure of workload, and other factors can compel workers to act against the company's best interests, resulting in chaos.

In a manufacturing plant there are often multiple work centers, one supplying another, which must all be synchronized to a common plan. Without coordination of those diverse activities, serious delays and other kinds of waste will result. Simply measuring the activities within any one of those work centers is not sufficient to keep the entire production flow moving in synchronization and harmony.

As an example, in one factory with multiple areas across several buildings, activities converted raw materials into components, which were ultimately delivered along with other materials to a final assembly department. One day the assembly department was setup to run a batch of products that was urgently needed to fill an order for one of our most important customers. Twelve assembly workers had taken up their positions. Tools and fasteners were at the ready. Components and other materials were all in place when one of the workers noticed a single type of component was missing. Without that one component assembly could not begin, so while twelve workers and their supervisors, along with a couple of QC inspectors at the end of the line, were all standing idle, the search was on for that missing part.

After confirming that is was not anywhere in the staging area before assembly, I went down to the machine room where those components were supposed to have been made. The machine that should have made that part the day before, was running at top speed producing other components. Upon reviewing the list of parts scheduled for that machine, we found the part we needed, and it was on the list before the part that was currently running. I asked the operator why this part was skipped over, and why the currently running parts were being produced even though they were not needed until a couple of days later.

His reply was that the missing part was a relatively small quantity, whereas the part now going through the machine was a nice long run. Since the machine operator knew his productivity was being measured based on parts per hour, the longer run made much more sense to him, which was why he decided to put off making the part assembly needed at that moment. From his point of view, he was being more productive favoring the larger runs, especially since setup of the machine took a long time. What difference would the small run make anyway?

That decision by a single machine operator, was catastrophic for the assembly department, and more importantly for, the sales order we needed to ship that afternoon. Like a lot of similar situations, this worker could not see the larger picture, instead focusing only on the throughput of his machine. This is a prime example of failure to operate based on an overall production schedule, instead looking only at the effects on the current work center.

From a cost accounting perspective, the machine room did great that day, while the assembly department was highly unproductive, wasting considerable labor, and falling behind on its output requirements. This is a prime example of how cost accounting on a department basis can completely skew the picture. Based on "efficiency values" expressed in dollars/hour, the machine department was in great shape, but something needed to be done to improve the assembly operation. The machine room supervisor had made his target for dollars of parts produced, whereas the assembly supervisor was questioned about why his department was holding up shipments again.

From the larger perspective, the company failed to meet its commitment to a key customer, costing precious good will and risking penalties for nonperformance which were part of our contract for that order.

A second example relates to the materials management issues we have already discussed earlier. In that same assembly department, many types of fasteners and hardware components were needed to build our products. One of those hardware items came in four individual parts from our supplier; a right and left for each drawer, and a mating right and left for the body of the product, all combined to become a drawer slide mechanism.

Since there were four separate packages each containing one of these components, each of which was added to the assembly at a different station on the line, and it was very common for quantities of the four parts to get out of balance. Often that was simply because a few would get misplaced on a bench or under a conveyor, or maybe a part was bad and set aside. Over time this imbalance actually caused a ripple effect through to the stockroom, because the assemblers would take each part separately as more were needed.

If this imbalance got very serious, it could shut down the line, since one missing part out of four brought production to a halt until the situation was corrected. These kinds of shortages happened routinely throughout the many subassembly and assembly departments in our plant.

This situation could even get bad enough that purchasing would be forced to order in odd quantities of these items, so that we could re-balance our stock. Of course that would also mean that we routinely wrote off certain inventory imbalances, which in the end reduced profit.

Again, the workers had no idea their behavior was resulting in costs and serious delays in the overall process. In fact they were all convinced that they were acting in the best interests of the company. Those people in purchasing were just failing to keep up with production!

Just like the machine operator, who was "cherry picking" his schedule to keep the machine throughput at the optimum level, these kinds of well-meaning behaviors were adding up to huge inefficiencies measured against our shipping requirements. But again, if we focused only on efficiency within a narrowly defined area, most of our work centers looked great. For some reason assembly keeps falling behind.

These problems can happen everywhere, even in the front office. Purchasing was also guilty of the same misjudgments, by working on the larger quantity orders first, or dealing with certain vendors, and leaving the other items for later. However, just one of those deferred items could be the part that stops production because it is not available when needed.

It is probably human nature to work on the larger issues first, and that behavior may seem like the most logical choice, outside the context of the company's overall schedule. Lacking the tools to put every task in the correct sequence and left to their own devices, people will act using their own best judgment. None of this is necessarily the result of any ill will or bad intent, it just happens. These behaviors are a source of chaos and disorder, all created innocently due to lack of guidance and proper prioritization of the tasks.

Reliable information systems are the basis for planning and coordination, especially as complexity increases. The larger and more complex the work environment, the more this natural chaos will occur. For this reason, it is never too early to begin getting your company's information in good working order. And like any preventive medicine, the longer you wait to start taking the cure, the more costly and painful it will be.

You Want It When?

The ability to commit to delivery dates is often key to winning business, and keeping those promised delivery dates is critical to maintaining good relationships.

Below we examine two different situations related to delivery commitments. The first one illustrates a problem with lead time in general, where every order had been taking too long from order-entry to delivery, and the entire sluggish fulfillment process was the issue.

The second example focuses on the problems with monitoring and controlling the production process. This is a case where the lack of reliable information had been costing orders. Without accurate and timely information, sales staff could not assure our customers of on-time delivery.

Fear of Loss

Our company was the prime supplier for hotel furniture of Holiday Inns. At the time, Holiday Inns had a division called Innkeepers Supply, which provided all the things a hotel needed, from napkins to furniture. To get into this favored position required meeting several criteria, which were the deciding factors in a semi-annual contract competition:

- **Design** - prototypes for new designs were submitted to Innkeepers, which had to meet their specifications for appearance and durability,

- **Price** - along with each design, we had to compete on price, with a total per-room maximum set by room category,

- **Delivery** - each competitor was expected to sign an agreement that guaranteed delivery of any new order, within a certain number of days. Failure to deliver by a specified date would result in per room, per diem penalties that were intentionally onerous.

The benefits of winning this competition were:

- 100% of the furniture needed for "parent company" rooms. The parent company, Holiday Inns, which at the time owned about 50,000 rooms, refurbished on a 7 year cycle, which meant we would get orders for approximately 7000 rooms per year under this deal.

- Since the winner would furnish the parent company rooms, the franchisees (more than double the parent company room total), would be very likely to buy the same designs from the selected vendor.

This was a huge amount of locked-in business, from the largest hotel chain in the world. So not only did we get the direct benefits from winning this contract, but we also had the prestige of being recognized as Holiday Inns' prime supplier. That recognition also led to considerable business from the other hotel chains. Clearly this was a contract that we were very anxious to maintain.

Our company had won this competition for years running. The designs we provided were cutting edge in terms of both appearance and durability. Our prices, and in the early stages, our delivery, were both acceptable as well.

Several of the previous war stories are from that plant. The production delays written about in those examples were not only costly, but were leading to potential cancellation of the contract. During that time period, Holiday Inns was going through an enormous growth cycle, building new hotels and refurbishing at an accelerating rate.

Prior to implementation of a comprehensive information system to manage our facility, as the order volume continued to increase, our deliveries began slipping beyond acceptable limits. Furthermore, as the company scrambled to improve, staff were added, machines were purchased, overtime became the norm, all resulting in higher costs of operation, but failing to fix the problem.

That single account had grown to about 40% of our entire annual volume, so losing it abruptly could potentially bankrupt our company. However, the strategies until that point amounted to throwing money at the problem, without any positive results. In fact, more machines, people, and overtime hours were all complicating our situation, making things far more difficult to manage. It was urgent that we find a new and successful approach.

At that moment in time, we bought a complete new computer system, some basic accounting, some database management tools (very basic), and contracted with a software development company to provide custom applications. The lead person over this purchase was the VP Sales and Marketing.

What were his priorities? The programming was all aimed at producing quoting and sales management tools of course. While everyone agreed that these were important tools, they did nothing to address our main problems of managing the order fulfillment process. Lead time had become the primary constraint on our growth.

Fortunately, the vendor contracted with for both hardware and software, was especially experienced with manufacturing systems. Although they could not put their time directly into the applications we needed, they were more than willing to help me design and plan the tools we so desperately needed for materials management and production control.

Within about 90 days we had created enough tools to start taking the pressure off our front office staff. Purchasing was first, where we developed our own MRP tools to plan the timing of our materials. At the same time, we implemented scheduling, so that we could start to overcome some of the problems with material storage and delivery to work centers. Scheduling and materials management are codependent activities, which if properly integrated and timed, will have a profound impact on throughput.

We added some very simple data collection tools which let us monitor and track the completion of each step of the manufacturing process.

Prior to all of this, everything had been on paper, and most timing decisions had been in the hands of the shop supervisors, whose database was a clipboard full of papers. We have already discussed how that situation was the cause of many of our delays.

With implementation of the new information systems, we were able to purchase more intelligently, allowing us to properly sequence the incoming materials, synchronized with our production demand.

Not only did we then have a much better grasp of timing, but we were also able to substantially reduce our total inventory by 40%. This reduction had the added benefit of making our warehouse easier to maintain and keep clean and organized. That result delighted the CEO and CFO, since the inventory reduction put $400,000 more cash in our bank account. Plus, insurance and many other maintenance and overhead costs were reduced similarly.

However the most important benefit was the improved flow of production. With the improved management systems, everything started flowing better. Workers were free of the previous burdens associated with managing their own schedules and incoming materials. These tasks were now done well by administrative and warehouse staff, so now production workers could focus all of their attention on quality and volume.

Our lead times came down dramatically, to the point where were no longer at risk of losing our prime contract with Holiday Inns. In fact we also turned results from the marginal profit numbers, into very respectable returns for the shareholders, all due to dramatic gains in productivity.

Hours had been reduced down to normal work weeks, without all the expensive overtime that was required before. That not only reduced costs, but also took pressure off of our overworked management and plant employees. Stress and overwork are leading contributors to mistakes and quality problems, so relieving the pressure also improved quality.

What machine purchase would have caused such positive results across the entire spectrum of our business? The company had already invested in more machinery than could be used efficiently, and that had not helped. More workers and scheduled time increased costs, but not productivity, with negative effects on quality.

It was simply the enabling effects of good data management that provided all these benefits in a very short time frame. With the proper tools to manage the flow of information, every department from the front office to the shop floor, and especially the warehouse, had become more effective, working in harmony.

Can We Take the Order?

In this second example, at another company making clocks for the consumer market, a similar problem was holding back growth. This company had wide national distribution though multiple channels of retail. The products were mostly wooden case clocks; grandfather, wall and mantel clocks, aimed at the mid to high end consumer.

These are products often given as gifts or to celebrate a holiday or special occasion. The retailers of such products like to promote them for occasions like father's day, mother's day, Thanksgiving, Christmas.

70

They would plan special advertising promotions, buying particular models that fit their objectives of style and price points.

A lot of money would be committed to advertising as well as inventory to prepare for the events. In planning these sales events, our customers would call to find out which models would be available for shipment in time for their promotion, and which ones would be available at special pricing. Our customer service staff needed know which models would be available at the time the sales event was planned, also dependent on the total order volume we were expecting from other dealers. These issues were beyond what any manual system could address.

If our dealers could not be assured of on time delivery of the models they wanted, they could not make the purchase. Without assurances that we could support their event, they might well choose to place an order with one of several competitors.

At the time, our company had very limited ability to confidently commit to deliveries under these circumstances, particularly when it was a seasonal event like a holiday. On hand inventory was fairly easy to keep track of, and even committing some of it to future orders was possible, but knowing for sure when the next batch of a particular model would be available, was much more difficult, much less predicting into the future with confidence. This weakness was causing us to lose substantial business.

It is one thing to be able to commit to shipping products that are in inventory, but another thing altogether to assure a dealer that his mix of products will be available at a specific future date.

This problem is one of planning and control, not production efficiency. With thousands of dealers — clock shops, retail furniture stores, discounters and department stores — nationwide, the complexity of the problem is too great for manual methods.

Many of the same solutions which were applied to solve production and inventory control issues, where also used to address the purchasing and materials management components of this dilemma. However, instead of a small number of customers buying in large volume, this dealer network was vast and required more finite controls for managing future demand and synchronizing production flow to match it, all without building excessive inventory!

Our planning and scheduling systems had to be much more sophisticated and accurate. For that to work, we also needed very strong monitoring of the production process (feedback) so that we could know for sure when each model would come off our production line. This was complicated by the fact that most of the clock mechanisms we used were mechanical, manufactured in Germany, requiring very careful handling and then a long testing phase for production, which was difficult to predict.

Our solution again leveraged our information systems, incorporating bar coded tags on each product that allowed us to monitor each individual clock through five phases of the production process, and then finally, shipment. The system had to be very easy to use and highly accurate. At the same time, we did not want to add any complications to the shop floor, since that might cause delays, which would run contrary to our primary goals.

In designing the solution, we also chose to incorporate our serial numbering and warrantee cards into the system, killing two birds with one stone. We therefore designed our tracking tag system to include the warrantee document with serial number, as the final component of tracking process.

The illustration on the next page shows a rough approximation of how all of this was done with a single paper "flow tag", which contained all of the tracking through multiple stages. It was also used at time of shipment, and left just the warrantee card attached to the back of the product.

Warrantee Details Clock Model # Clock Serial # Warrantee Contact Information	
Mail-in Warrantee Card	
Shipment	‖‖‖‖‖ ‖‖‖‖ ‖‖‖ ‖‖‖ ‖‖‖‖ ‖‖
Final Pack	‖‖‖‖‖ ‖‖‖‖ ‖‖‖ ‖‖‖ ‖‖‖ ‖‖
Pre Pack	‖‖‖‖‖ ‖‖‖‖ ‖‖‖ ‖‖‖ ‖‖‖ ‖‖
Testing	‖‖‖‖‖ ‖‖‖‖ ‖‖‖ ‖‖‖ ‖‖‖ ‖‖
Assembly	‖‖‖‖‖ ‖‖‖‖ ‖‖‖ ‖‖‖ ‖‖‖ ‖‖

The top section of this example was the part that at the end of the process that would remain on the product as the customers reference. This component contained the short form of our warrantee, along with the model #, serial #, and customer service contract information.

The second component down, was our mail-in card that the customer would use to register the product. Perforations below these two components would allow workers to remove the tracking section upon shipment.

The lower five sections were used to track the product through every step of the production process, plus the shipment. These tags were used in order from the bottom up, starting with assembly and progressing through the final packaging stage. The clock would then be put into inventory until an order was processed.

When the product was ordered, the item would be pulled from inventory and staged at the shipping dock. When the truck was loaded, the final bar code "Shipment" would be scanned, which caused that serial-numbered item to be added to the packing list.

Each of these scans represented several activities in a routing, but we didn't need that level of detail for this type of tracking. We were simply counting completions through certain key count-points that provided management and sales staff information about what products were moving through production, and when they should become available.

This simple flow tag system captured all the critical status information as each product moved though our factory, making it much easier for our sales order department to see exactly which products were available, and even which ones were moving through the production process, soon to be ready for shipment.

It also consolidated the identification of the product (model and serial number), with the warrantee processing, and all the manufacturing tracking steps we needed to improve the visibility of the production process against our schedule.

With these tracking features, our sales and customer service processes were greatly improved. They could easily see the flow of products through the entire pipeline leading to finished goods.

Of course this information was also extremely useful for many other aspects of production management as well. The ability to easily track each step of the process helped us improve the workflow, because we had meaningful statistics on which models and which processing steps were holding back our throughput.

This solution consolidated several individual steps, greatly reducing our costs and potential for errors; a synergistic quality. The most valuable result was the flow tracking data, which cost almost nothing to collect, but helped us in multiple ways across several departments of our company.

We solved our initial problem, enabling our sales staff to predict delivery times much more accurately. That single benefit allowed us to avoid the previous pitfalls, where we had been unable to commit to our dealers in order to support their special sales events.

This is also an example of how merging several process steps can yield substantial cost savings, over multiple processes; synergy at work.

Left Behind

There is an appropriate analogy that applies well to the importance of keeping pace with changes in technology, particularly new capabilities that result in a competitive advantage:

Keeping up with technology is like padding a canoe up stream...

... stop padding and you will drift backward.

Microsoft made its first well-recognized mistake when they concluded that the Internet was a fad. It did not take long for competitors to demonstrate that error, and then Microsoft was forced to play catch-up.

Our example is also related to the Internet, which as we all now know, has become the platform for major improvements in processing sales orders. Gone are the days of paper-based catalogs, and even the Yellow Pages are no longer printed. We all shop online today for almost anything we need. This is true at home and in businesses, but how many businesses today are really taking advantage of Web commerce?

One of the larger companies I have worked with over the years, has multiple product lines all sold through a national dealer network of home improvement centers. This manufacturer specializes in premium products for luxury homes, including flooring, doors and entry features, and custom hardwood mouldings. Each of these product lines has different options and can be configured in almost infinite combinations of materials and design elements.

Several years ago, this company began to realize that its dealer network was eroding in one of their product segments; not because of reduced demand, not due to quality or even pricing, but simply because the process of placing an order was too complicated and slow.

Due to the immense number of features and options, the dealers were required to fill out forms with all the specifications, and then wait for a quotation. Because of those manual methods, there were also many possible mistakes that could easily cause serious problems if the order was placed. Mistakes could mean even further delay, especially if they were caught after shipment, which would often require remanufacture of the order.

This painful process was frustrating and costly for both the manufacturer and the dealer network, and was resulting in substantial erosion of good will.

Competitors were taking notice of this weakness, with a few moving to Web-based order processing. The key to processing such complicated orders online was an emerging technology tool now referred to as an order configurator. A configurator is simply an onscreen entry form, listing all of the features and options, such that customers can quickly make their selections, let the system calculate the price, and then if the price is acceptable, place the order. All of this process takes place quickly, in real time, without the need for the manufacturer to respond.

My manufacturing customer was watching their dealer network shrink, simply because competitors were able to provide this type of Web commerce site, which was quickly becoming the expected method for so many kinds of order processing.

To add to the problem, the product line in question (custom interior mouldings), required a visual presentation of the configured items, particularly since luxury home builders often used multiple mouldings in combinations to achieve the look they wanted. Therefore, the order configurator had to provide an image of the selected products, all grouped together as the design required, so that the total package could be confirmed to meet appearance and dimensional specifications.

This company offers a large number of different profiles that can be ordered separately or grouped into collections that achieve the desired look for each room. These are all offered in a wide range of wood species as well. So, the objective was to create a configurator that not only priced the products quickly and accurately, but also would allow the user to manipulate the various profiles into groups, with a visual display of the result on screen.

This type of visual Web commerce site is far more complex to build than a simple SKU-based order processing system. However, this is exactly the kind of functionality that today's consumers are coming to expect.

These were the goals as this project began. The company already had a robust database management system to support the range of features and options, as well as the pricing requirements. Each individual moulding product also had a CAD drawing associated with it, providing the starting point for the visual component of the configurator.

Web design tools today also offer capabilities to create this type of visual functionality on top of all the data management activities to calculate the prices as selections are made. With the underlying data structures providing all of the elements we needed, and with the visualization tools, we set to work designing and creating the new visual configurator.

This is not easy, nor is such a configurator inexpensive. But with the diminishing sales volume continuing to slide, as well as concerns about dealer confidence, the costs were considered necessary. The investment decision was made, simply to stop the erosion of business in this important product line. They set a goal of just keeping the competition at bay, and avoiding the continued loss of dealers.

Upon launching the new Web commerce site, and promoting its features to their dealer network, the company was pleased with the positive reaction. The configurator was designed to make selection and arrangement of the components easy, with drag-and-drop functionality for positioning the individual mouldings. As selections were made, the prices would be instantly calculated. At the end of the process, the dealer would have a printable or email version of each grouping, with the specifications and pricing neatly organized for presentation to the builder and homeowner.

After only a few months of operation, the new system had easily achieved the goal to stemming the losses, as well as causing an increase in this product category. Moreover, the company began to track an amazing and unexpected benefit; old customers that had moved on to other vendors were in fact returning.

Dealers were so delighted with the vastly improved visual order processing capabilities that they began promoting these products to their customers. Gone was the pain and difficulty of the old cumbersome ordering process. New projects could be designed and quoted instantly, resulting in more business for the manufacturer, their dealers, as well as the home builder's those dealers cultivated.

The new visual configurator based Website was such a success that the manufacturer began telling the industry about their technological breakthrough. They were gushing with pride as their dealer network and industry peers recognized the leadership and foresight of this innovation. Even today, after the several years of operation that have past, this company is still crediting this one investment as a key to their turnaround from the low point after the collapse of the residential housing market.

Paddle your technology canoe as fast and hard as possible, and rewards will be great. Stop paddling and the costs to catch up may be unbearable.

Explosive Growth

What business owner doesn't want more sales volume?

What sales manager worth his salt isn't striving for rapid improvement in his numbers?

Your company has labored and invested heavily in new products and services, planned the marketing, and rolled out the promotions, now what do you do when the wave of orders rolls in? Can you respond to the surge in demand this wave puts on your order fulfillment processes from sales to production and shipping?

Sometimes a great opportunity presents itself, whether planned and executed over years, or as an unexpected break that must be taken advantage of quickly. However it comes about, your company needs to be prepared to respond appropriately, to make the most of every potential for growth.

The Home-Run Opportunity
While working for a consumer products manufacturer, we were presented with such an opportunity, not only to close a huge sale, but to have several such waves of business flowing in over the next couple of years. The price and terms were very favorable; on paper we stood to grow sales by double digits. Of course the only catch was the commitment to deliver an extremely large quantity of a specific product over a very short time period, with stiff penalties for failure.

We were pioneering a new marketing trend with one of the top names in the industry: American Express. Their VP of Marketing had envisioned a major additional income stream on top of all the credit card processing and membership fees.

The revolutionary idea was simple: along with the credit card statements sent out to their 30 million members each month, include advertising for merchandize. Today, assuming you still receive paper statements, the inclusion of advertising with your bill is typical, but at that time American Express was breaking new ground. To make it even more compelling, the card member simply checked a box and returned the coupon with that month's payment, and the product would be shipped and billed in 12 payments on the subsequent statements. What could be easier?

Since American Express customers were considered to be in the higher income/spending segment of the market, the merchandize would be premium. Our product was at the $1000 price point ($999 to be exact), which they considered a nice maximum to get started. The "roll out" strategy was for three mailing cycles, each one to different groups of cardholders, a few weeks apart in time. The total targeted number of units sold was 7000, or about $7,000,000 in gross sales dollars per roll out.

From our perspective, the pressure of producing 7000 units over an expected 90 day period, with the largest surge in the first of three cycles, presented some major problems in manufacturing and shipping. This promotion would add volume on top of everything else we were doing, and we did not want to jeopardize our existing customer relationships for a short term surge. But who could pass up the chance to transact so much additional business with one of the most recognized brand names in the world, and especially with a company known to pay its bills?

This was a dream opportunity which we accepted whole-heartedly, immediately beginning the design and planning stages to ensure success. We were able to meet this challenge because our company had already invested in information systems, which were designed and implemented to support wide swings in volume. We were a company serving a highly seasonal market that ebbed and flowed with holidays and other seasonal events.

We had learned to adapt and manage those ups and downs, all while maintaining control over investments in inventory and production. One approach to such a huge surge might be to build all the products in advance, but we lacked the cash, the physical space, and the mindset to follow that course. Plus we had to maintain inventory and production flow to support all of our regular customers, so building only one product over a long period was not an option.

This is where we see the true benefits of flexible planning and scheduling systems. Without the ability to rapidly simulate future conditions, accurate scheduling of production output is not possible. The dynamics are numerous and complex. Every material and capacity constraint must be considered, or the plan might be doomed by a few shortages.

The old "common sense" thinking might suggest building inventories on components to create large buffers against these potential shortages. However, again we did not have the capital or the warehouse space to allow for such buffers. We have also seen how there are many other hidden costs to building inventory, including: damage, imbalances, handling costs, insurance, and on. Large inventories actually encumber rather than support good production flow.

Without the information system we had carefully implemented earlier, this home-run opportunity would either have been passed up, or if accepted would have severely overloaded production. The carrying costs of building inventory to avoid late shipment, would have been beyond our credit lines, plus would have added significant interest expenses.

In our case, we were able to project demand over time, across the full range of materials and capacity constraints. Working with our vendors, we got them to commit to specific volumes, delivered just in time, as the surges in demand rose and fell. Internally, our production capacity was highly scalable. We were able to increase most assembly processes, simply by adding parallel lines, fed by the same material delivery systems running at higher rates. Our ability to grow and shrink production capacity was all part of our ongoing process improvement efforts, since that sort of flexibility is a key component necessary to compete in consumer markets.

The only way to successfully manage such an explosive surge in business, is to have a strong supporting structure of well organized information and tools to use that data to manage the resources and activities.

Some Conclusions

Give people good information and good decisions will follow. The converse is almost always true; bad information leads to bad decisions. The ability to collect and put information to good use, all in real-time, is essential to keeping sharp and competitive.

Part of what makes for high quality information is that it is well organized, free of erroneous or duplicate records, and it is stored in the most efficient manner for fast access.

If your company develops a strategy, which first considers your data as the foundation for all the processes that manage your business, then whatever you want to build on top of that foundation—for selecting and sorting, calculations, and presentation of that information—will all be within reach.

Everything has a cost, therefore it is important to consider how much data is needed and is reasonable to collect. Simplification of the processes throughout your business will also be possible, once the data requirements are very clear.

Explosive Growth

In many cases unnecessary information is being routinely collected and saved, when in fact this data will never be used for any meaningful purpose. Collecting unneeded information is wasteful and can be a source of frustration to employees, who are already under pressure to perform tasks that add value.

Review the overall processes throughout your entire business, and see how they can work together. Then you will start to see the synergies, available by way of connections to a common set of data.

Part II: Divide and Conquer - Finding the Cures

This part provides guidelines on how to simplify the core problems and then plan and administer the cures. In totality, major information systems implementations touch almost every facet of a business. This is especially true today with so many connection options compared to the past where things were typically limited to just local or wide area business networks, primarily connecting office staff.

Plans for transitioning from old to new affect each area of a company in different ways. Therefore, a realistic implementation plan takes these special needs into consideration, in terms of timing as well as the particular setup, configuration, and training each functional area will require.

Typically, sales people rely heavily on the customer relationship management (CRM) side of their company's information system. Sales needs to manage the flow of leads and suspects into prospects, quotations, and hopefully, customers and orders. That sales process is a sub-system within ERP, and will usually be high on the list of features for improvement.

Tools to help manage the sales process, leading to increased business, often become the main focus; however it is important to prepare a logical, step by step plan for the implementation of your new system. A building must be constructed from the ground up, not the top down. Similarly, the task of planning the sequence and dependencies of each implementation step is crucial, and care in planning and execution will result in a strong system that can be completed as rapidly and error-free as possible.

With the range of technologies available today, upgrading elements of the sales process will prove highly rewarding. Some of the best high-tech options are costly and take a huge amount of planning, but the pay back can be significant and in some cases extremely rapid.

While at first glance it may not appear that a huge amount of improvement can be expected on the CRM side, the benefits from the interconnections that our relational database system provides are time-saving at a minimum, and life changing in many cases. Every company has customer and vendor data that includes names, addresses, and so forth, so what are the benefits from putting all of that into a new database?

The key is in how the data is organized and accessed. With well structured information of any kind, finding what is needed becomes faster and easier. Sorting through disorganized records for the critical bit of information can be frustrating and painfully slow. The benefits of having almost instant access, selecting and presenting the required information with a few mouse clicks, becomes an enormous asset and a powerful tool in itself for any sales team. A well designed and implemented CRM can have profound impact, freeing sales staff to focus on the process of closing business, rather than searching for the name of some prospect.

Of course there will also be many features made available that were not even possible in the legacy system. There are better ways to organize and view information, schedule important tasks and events, and many new capabilities in managing all of the steps in the sales process. Your system should also be able to store and manage all of the related documents that are important, such as, emails, Word docs, spreadsheets, and so on, which although created by other software, should still be connected through your CRM system. These documents should be easily accessible and opened with a mouse click when needed.

Also standard tools such as Microsoft Outlook should be integrated into your user interface, rather than having to work between these applications separately. Tasks set in the ERP system for example, should automatically show up on your Outlook calendar.

The other important work you can do to improve the sales process, is to make quoting and ordering more accurate and free of mistakes. These symptoms can be very painful, and curing them will not only make the process more efficient, but also open the channels of sales opportunities flowing into your sales hopper.

There are many tools in your new system to assist with this work, from parametric product structures, to Web commerce with photo-realistic 3D imaging of custom configured and priced products. The range of solutions is broad, and we will provide the basic knowledge to help make the selections and plan the entire implementation process. Concepts covered will range from building the appropriate data structures, to choosing the methods to improve quoting and order processing throughout your distribution network.

Today customers want things their way, so make-to-order is becoming far more common and in some cases necessary to remain competitive. The days of "any color you want as long as it's black" are long gone. Flexibility to provide the latest features and options, not only help get the orders in the first place, but also allow the manufacturer to produce the items at higher margins.

Then there is the manufacturing itself. The core of your business, the reflection of your company's identity, the products and services that have distinguished your brand, will be found in your products and processes that create them. Your new ERP system will be a powerful toolset, enabling a transformation in the way information is collected, stored, presented for decision making.

In any manufacturing operation—whatever the strategy or production philosophy from make-to-stock mass production, to just in time (JIT), or engineered-to-order—accurate timing of the materials, components, processing activities, and availability of physical space and machines, are all key factors in maintaining the highest productivity.

In simple broad terms, these conditions are required:

- *the right things,*

- *in the right places,*

- *at precisely the right times*

...or productivity suffers.

The following chapter is named for this idea, and continues on in that vein to identify the primary objectives for your implementation strategy.

As with the sales process, just organizing and interconnecting manufacturing data will result in vast improvements. And that foundation is just the starting point, because armed with these tools you can streamline every kind of activity throughout all of the operations. The data will be the most useful tool set of all.

The information systems underlying your manufacturing processes are the infrastructure supporting all the activities—direct and indirect— that determine the quality and quantity of your total output. The best materials, machines, and manpower resources are wasted if they are not coordinated with the flow, in harmony with your production schedule. Good control and coordination of the many interlinked processes, leads to high-quality, at the lowest possible cost.

Building the best information system to support all of this requires a good organization of the processes involved and the data needed to support them. Once you know the components you need for your system, they must be put in logical sequence, with careful planning to use your precious resources wisely, maximizing results while minimizing waste. Yes, even the implementation of software systems is subject to the processes of lean thinking.

These kinds of results are only possible through sincere commitment to your implementation strategy and by management consistently providing the resources necessary. However, the costs can often be spread over the implementation process to a degree, and the payback from a well-crafted plan will be rapid.

The key as with any investment, is to plan well and buy right, with specific ROI targets. Also as just mentioned, be very careful not to spend too soon on, training, setup, and custom features. These are precious budgeted resources, which if used too early in the process, will be wasted.

However, do not despair... help is on the way. The chapters that follow will establish useful guidelines to achieve these difficult goals and in the process acquire the basic skills to continue making improvements.

The huge number of tasks may look impossible, so think in terms of the popular saying:

> *"how do you eat and elephant?"*...

> *"one bite at a time!"*

Careful organization of the work makes the job much less painful and provides results more quickly. In fact, it is often possible to begin reaping returns early in the process, by attacking the steps in the implementation plan in the most logical order. This concept is covered in a later chapter.

Therefore, this section is comprised of a series of chapters devoted to simplifying and organizing an information system implementation plan; from data structures, through the user interfaces that collect and present that precious information.

The following chapters are intended to present the key concepts for a step-by-step process, which leads to a solid connected structure to support your business. There will also be discussion about the features of the software, including application interface consistency, data collection methods, as well as customizable views and dashboards.

The common thread is the process of simplification, which is the first major topic. This is followed by a high level view of database design, and object oriented programming; just some concepts worth knowing when considering the foundations of your new information system. Our objective is to provide the foundations of these technologies, without getting bogged down in too many details.

The later chapters discuss the importance of taking ownership, organizing your implementation team, and balancing the workload.

Our final chapter in this part is an outline of the major components of an implementation plan, providing a template for your specific project. Our conclusion is a recap of the benefits that can be expected from a fully functioning system.

Our objectives provide the most synergistic results:

- a solid database foundation,

- full range of data collection options,

- easily customized presentation of the information,

- connectivity between other networks, hardware, & applications,

- all with the flexibility to adapt to constant change

Right Thing, Right Place, Right Time

This chapter begins the how-to part, where we will apply some logic to reduce complex problems down into manageable problems, solved using the simplification techniques we will be presenting.

The best way to start any project is to clearly list the objectives. The specific details of your objectives, will of course vary from our examples, but there will be many important principles that will help guide any system implementation process. Throughout the chapters in part one, we saw a number of examples of the problems that arose in growing businesses, followed by some solutions and how they were applied in those cases. What general principles can we derive from those scenarios?

Timing is everything... and that is certainly the case for managing all of the resources to keep production flowing, for example.

Time is money..and that has a multiplying effect when just a few missed items can stop an entire production order.

This chapter is named for one of the most fundamental guiding principles in work flow improvement. The overriding imperative is: keep supplying the right resources, in the right places where they will be needed, delivered at exactly the right time. Any variation from such consistent flow causes delay, wasting resources and impeding overall throughput.

Leave out just one material needed, or put it in the wrong place, deliver it late or deliver components simply in the wrong order... the list of costly problems goes on.

The point is that synchronization in the flow of all resources is a critical objective for any manufacturing company, and many other types of business as well. We have also seen that these timing problems are not solved by adding excess resources such as, building up larger inventories, buying more equipment, or increasing staff. Those kinds of remedies are wasteful at best, and can often lead to impeding the flow, which is the exact opposite of the result you want.

With regard to data management, you are also seeking to avoid the old "islands of information" approach, where even though we employ many useful applications, they are all disconnected from each other. Since no one software package will provide 100% of the needed functionality, we may never be as seamlessly integrated as some might want. However, with a capable and open database system as our platform, connections to other tools are usually possible.

The specialized application software packages that you need for specific activities such as, engineering drawings, CNC code generation, graphics tools, etc., will all stay in the mix. An ERP system does not attempt to provide these kinds of special functionality that vertical market products do so much better. However, what we can do is create links between the ERP platform data, and the special data generated or needed by those other applications.

These customized links to the ERP database may be costly endeavors, but once functioning, such links eliminate islands that would otherwise continue to be an impediment to the work flow.

Your new integrated solution should allow you to select and tailor different types of application software, all sharing common data, facilitated by a central database. That database will have the ability to import and export data, formatted as each external application requires.

Achieving your objectives requires a network of data connections between all kinds of processes. This network must be engineered to support the business activities as you see them today, and allow for constant changes in the nature and organization of the processes connected to your network. You need an information systems grid, providing access to data storage and retrieval hardware, and facilitating the flow of all needed data for each process; delivering the right things, to the right places, at the right times.

That describes some of the internal infrastructure, everything in the local area network (LAN), and this grid facilitates external connections as well. Managed, secured, connections to the Internet, WIFI, email accounts, FTP sites, special connections for dealers, all of these kinds of connections will be better managed when the overall scope of this enterprise grid is mapped out as part of the implementation strategy.

Today we see enterprise systems, with users connected by an ever increasing array of options, from direct LAN connection to smartphones used by field service teams to capture jobsite costs. Tablet computers are another way to keep workers connected while they are outside the office network environment. No doubt there will continue to be innovations in communication hardware and mobile computing. As long as your grid is capable of adding and upgrading these kinds of features, you will not be left out of any of these technology advancements.

All of these types of connectivity are well within the scope of current ERP system technology, and should certainly be on your checklist. Even if these access methods are not be immediately needed, future requirements must be considered to ensure the functionality is available when it is needed. This is not rocket science, it is standard stuff for today's servers and client/server database systems.

Looking at the problem architecturally, you will need a foundation comprised of a database management system that can support the current and future loads our business activities will present. These loads are measured in terms of the various kinds of data, the volumes of data, and the speed with which that information will need to flow in order to keep up with your work flow demands.

Data Grid

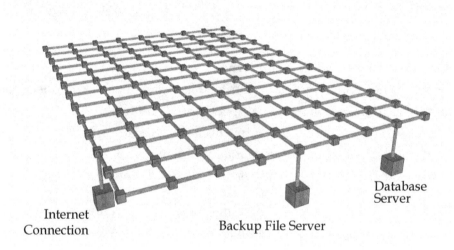

Internet Connection

Backup File Server

Database Server

This foundation can be viewed as a network or grid, able to supply connections across all of the processes plugged into it. At this point in our graphic, we see servers connected below the grid as a portal to the storage and server-based processing components of the system.

With all of your data available over such a broad spectrum of possible connections, your system will have the flexibility to respond to your needs, current and future.

This network also provides a common connection to the Internet. With this underlying structure as the foundation to your system, you can see how easy it will be to snap on additional components which will allow access to your data grid.

Connected To The Grid

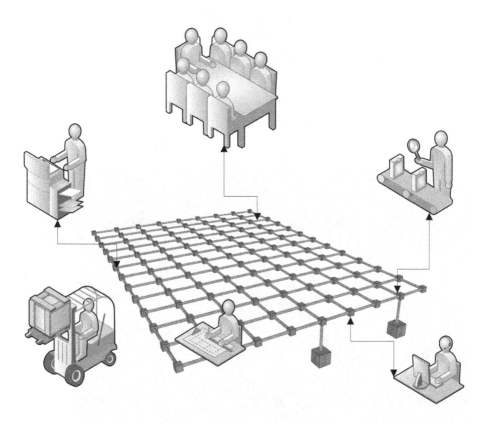

The result is a bit like a utility infrastructure, serving a region with power and communication resources. In a similar manner, your data grid must be capable of expanding and changing in response to changing demand.

As any electrical engineer knows, it is not a simple task to manage all of these connections and the data traffic that will result, since the demand may change dramatically from one part of the grid to another. Fortunately in our current information systems world, that particular problem has been solved by a number of available client/ server database management systems.

The hardware to manage LAN and Internet connections today are relatively low-cost and easy to setup and use. Another option growing in popularity is hosted servers or cloud servers, which take full responsibility for the hardware and up time, in exchange for a monthly fee. Such systems also provide tools to manage security, backup and restore, user rights and permissions, controls over outside access, and changes to the data structures.

As long as you are building your structures on a suitable database system, and on the correct hardware, then your platform should be adequate to meet your needs. However, selecting the platform components only provides the grid structure to support the system you will construct.

Next you will need to design the data structures and organization to get your system up and running, fully reflecting your real world data requirements across all facets of your business.

A great deal of that organization and connectivity will be furnished as a starting point if your company purchases an ERP system, but there will still be many choices to make as to how your data structures will take shape to meet your specific needs.

Nothing is perfect out of the box, so plan for the necessary customization. Verify that whatever you buy, you will have capabilities for customization.

Even if your company purchases a system, there should be a large amount of latitude with regard to the design of the user interfaces, product configurators, presentation tools, and so on. If this is not the case, you are starting out with a severe handicap. Such user interface features and options should be considered very carefully, since they are the points of intersection with your data grid.

To provide unrestricted flow of information to and from your activities, these interfaces must be built for easy, error free, and responsive operation by the intended users. Since this is part of the ongoing improvement of all processes, the ability to modify user interface components is a very important criterion on your system selection checklist.

One more essential component to consider when planning a systems implementation project: the training, support, and general encouragement necessary to keep your team focused and fully able to complete all the tasks they will be assigned as the work progresses. If your company is purchasing a system, then be sure that the seller has adequate service capabilities to support your efforts in a timely manner.

It is of course equally important that your company is firmly committed to the work and to providing all of the necessary resources.

Your team will need a lot of support, in the form of:

- advice on the selection of proper hardware

- installation of components on network servers and client machines

- initial setup of databases

- import and data entry processes to load the data

- customization of interface components, configurators, data connections

- training at all levels from system administration to user level

This list is just the highlights of the kinds of service and support that are typically needed to get a system up and running in a reasonable time frame.

Many companies follow the false logic, that costs could be lowered by trying some of this without spending money on outside technicians and other support resources. Nothing could be further from the truth. Although there are many tasks where you should definitely do yourself, that does not mean you should omit the important training and support services that experienced technicians can provide. This is particularly true with regard to initial setup, but we do not mean tasks like data entry and organization, which your internal team needs to do.

The chapter named DIY discusses some of the kinds of work that should be assigned to the participants within your company, and distinguishes those from tasks that would be better left to more experienced professionals. It is extremely important that everyone — internal team and hired guns — are pulling in the same direction, with full buy-in to the project plan and its objectives. As with any such endeavor, that issue is one of good management and leadership.

To state the major implementation objectives:

1. Select a database platform that provides the functionality to support our information needs for the foreseeable future. The architecture must be a robust, client/server system, with SQL access.

2. Organize the major data structures for an accurate representation and full support of your activities.

3. Design and build interfaces and methods for users to quickly and efficiently find or input the data, with the least interference to the processes.

4. Provide training and support for the users, which encourages a high level of buy-in, and allows for constructive feedback for constant improvement of the system.

The chapters that follow address these issues in greater detail, breaking out the separate topics, proceeding step by step from the data structures, through the interface tools, and implementation methods to achieve your objectives, on time and on budget.

The most important priority will be doing the implementation right the first time. Every complex project involves some wasted effort, back tracking and reworking the plan, because certain details were not considered. The costs of such delays can be very high, however, these problems can be avoided through study and careful planning.

While this book may not contain the detailed answers to every possible question, it does provide the guidelines and structure needed to build your company's own successful implementation plan with realistic and achievable milestones.

The goal is no less than total control over the flow of information that drives your company.

Right thing, Right place, Right time.

It all begins with learning to simplify.

Simplify

There are lots of popular methodologies that are taught today for the purpose of increasing the efficiency of any kind of process we might encounter. Lean, Kaizen, 6-Sigma, Theory of Constraints... the list goes on. Much of this relies heavily on math and statistical control methods. We will leave all that to others and take a more conceptual approach.

Those disciplines are all systematic processes for organizing teams to solve problems by rooting out waste. This book is not intended as a course in any of those, but we will, from time to time, point out a few of their key concepts that are useful in achieving our objectives.

As a subset of lean, I like a process called 5-S which stands for:

- Sort (know what you have)

- Straighten (organize it)

- Shine (keep it clean)

- Standardize (so everyone can use it)

- Sustain (keep it up, do not get sloppy)

These principles were developed as methods for the improvement of physical things, but the same approach works well for your data. 5-S is a very simple way of thinking about a continuous process of refinement. The same kind of refinement process applies to configuration of data structures for optimum speed and capabilities.

In fact, there is a refinement process that software developers call *"database normalization"* which follows similar thinking to ensure that resulting data structures are the most efficient and reliable. The basics of this process are so important that the next chapter is devoted to a few of those concepts.

Early on in mathematics, we were taught to simplify equations in order to make them easier to solve. Our brains grasp things better if issues can be distilled down into their most elemental form. It is easier to see logical patterns when the information is well ordered and clear.

Since our brains also do better with images than words, a graphical representation is often helpful. This is one reason why flow charting business processes remains a powerful tool for clarifying the apparent complexities. Graphical presentation highlights problems, allowing the potential options for improvements to be visualized. Flow patterns that clearly waste resources become more apparent, and potentially better patterns may be envisioned.

It is a bit like looking at a map and realizing there is a much simpler or shorter route that eliminates backtracking and redundancies. Without such a high-level view, those options might not have been noticed. There are many forms of flow charting, and we will use just a bit of it to help explain the structural aspects and relationships in databases. We will also use flow charting to map out production processing steps and their relationships to timing of materials. And we will use graphic representations of our data communications network to help visualize the nature and scope of our system.

In general, graphics are great tools for stating and solving problems of all kinds, and can be used in many applications.

On the following page is a simple flowchart representing some of the major processes found in a typical make-to-order manufacturing company. Like most businesses, everything starts with a sales process.

Simplify

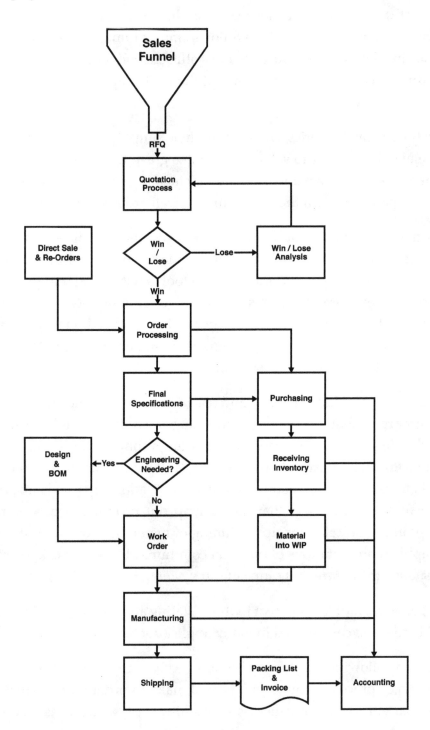

This example begins with collecting sales opportunities through a process with a sales funnel graphic at the top of the flow chart. The first step after an opportunity is received is a quotation, which either wins or loses the sales order. If lost we have a sub process for analysis of the quotation to learn why the bid was lost.

A win starts the order processing phase, which triggers purchasing, final specifications, engineering, and all the steps through manufacturing and shipping.

Purchasing flows into inventory and project materials allocations into work-in-progress (WIP).

Everything involving money flows through to accounting as well, where the financial results are recorded and presented to management for decision making.

This example is a view from a high-level, one that is helpful when thinking in terms of overall flow of information between some of the major processes. This is the best level at which to begin, and helps shape the process as details are filled in at the sub-levels.

In later examples we will see a little more detail in process flow charting of some production activities. In many cases, this kind of flow charting can involve different levels of granularity, with big picture views, and then zoomed in views expanding on the details.

With the business processes charted out in broad strokes (don't try to include every step of every process), visualizing your data requirements also becomes easier. Each one of those boxes on your chart calls out for the data needed to do that activity, make that decision, and convey that information.

Also the data needed to control and report on the processes is clearly evident as you examine the flow. Selecting the optimum points to monitor progress is also easier to visualize, and even the immediate need for change in the flow can become obvious. These are all great objectives, but how do we get there?

As with the discussion about data structures earlier, simplification has enormous benefits. Mapping out the data structures helps optimize and validate the design. Again using a variation of the 5-S approach, this procedure lets us start with a fresh assessment of the components we have defined, and the system implementation process provides the perfect opportunity to straighten and clean.

So if we are looking to simplify, it would make sense to start by first identifying the basic building blocks and the properties of each component. This approach will also result in a common set of objects we can use to create the flow charts or other representations of our processes.

We have used the term "element" in its general meaning; the simplest form of something. What we will discuss now is how we define the elements, structures built by in combination with other elements, and finally the difference between templates and reality.

These are all important concepts to understand, if you plan to leverage your investment in information. This knowledge is not intended to direct the reader toward building a system from scratch. However, just as a basic understanding of math, physics, and chemistry provide the foundational knowledge for solving many practical problems, in this work there are some basic sciences.

Studying these fundamental sciences we also learned to employ logic for problem solving. Most of us got the first formal training in the principles of logic, when studying plain geometry (Euclidean) in high school, when we had to learn to do "proofs" using only solid facts.

Just as a basic understanding of the forces (power), particles (material things), and the many interactions between them, forms the basis for learning more complex ideas, so do we need some common ground and definitions for the forces and material things we work with to make money.

Forces

In physics, the things that embody energy are forces that usually hold physical things together or push them apart. These forces are among the fundamental components or building blocks we have to work with. In the business world, the smallest, most basic force we define is in terms of currency, referring to money. To mirror that property, our objects will all carry a cost attribute, which will be the basis for any planning or financial transactions.

Forces can produce work: energy applied with a result (usually movement). Current physics describes more than one force and that gets more complicated all the time. However, business is, thankfully, much simpler. In business the force we apply is money, which similar to physics, may or may not be used efficiently. And just like in budgeting, we need a unit of measure that works for everything we will do, which in the US is usually the dollar, but most ERP systems handle conversions and multi-currency environments as well.

Therefore, continuing in this vein, every element we will define will have an associated energy (cost/value), expressed in dollars. Everything has some value, no matter how large or small it is. A non-zero amount is required for any transaction to occur. Everything has cost.

This force is the essence of what businesses seek. It is the money that is invested (or wasted), spent on the materials, labor, and overhead, to build the products you sell. So this force — money, capital — is very important to watch over and manage wisely. We need an accurate accounting of how our funds are invested, so that our managers can conserve precious resources and optimize results. Those results will be the profit that remains after all the costs have been collected and totaled. The money is the essential force to track.

Maybe the physics analogy is getting a bit stretched here, but this way of mentally envisioning a "property" and its value as an attribute of every incremental object we set out to manage, is useful if we really want to envision the leanest path.

Nothing is handled in your business without costs, therefore, if we accept that there is a value for everything, and look at all of the building blocks, each with their associated costs, we have a much better vantage point for making the best decisions. This kind of thought process will put your management in greater control, focused on the proper metrics to squeeze the most out of the available resources.

Elements

Next let us consider the components that we can use to build the structures we will make. These are the smallest building blocks that we have to make our products; all the resources, described using the smallest common denominator.

- Materials - raw, supplies and expendables

- Manpower (Activity) - direct, indirect

- Machines - resources and assets of all kinds

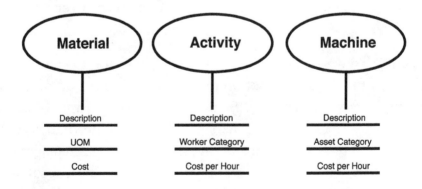

Our data definitions must describe these elements with all of the necessary attributes; description, cost/value, etc., such that products made from them will have the correct value. With such compact and well normalized elements, we can build the structures we can rely on with confidence.

We chose these three elements because these categories are typical and with their attributes can carry all the information we will need these objects to store. In fact these elements are the containers that hold the details about everything we do in the manufacturing processes.

The material element is the one most understood, and thus taken for granted in many cases. This element contains the details about just one unique item, which is purchased in this condition from a supplier. We will not get into the details of serial and lot tracking or other features of this object; in these examples we will only use the material element for building and costing some simple products.

Activity is something that implies some sort of work, either directly contributing to the manufacturing process, or indirectly as in supporting services. In many systems, only direct activities would be used in a routing or product structure, with other costs contributed as overhead factors.

The last element is even more vague, but is critical for more than just costing. I can represent anything of significant value, from a simple tool to complex collections of production machinery. With this element we can describe the flow of a process and how certain resources affect throughput.

Any of the elements can be a constraint on throughput, which means they may govern the maximum flow rate to which the entire process will be limited. This information can allow certain scheduling systems to calculate completion dates.

There are also areas within your facility called work centers, that can carry costs and impose constraints on flow. These are not direct components of the product structure, but they help define flow patterns and points for data collection, material delivery, and other resource requirements. We will later see how using the concept of work centers, will help us capture costs, using simple data collection methods based on where something is in the process.

These are the primary elements most manufacturing systems will use to represent the components of cost and constraints on workflow, which will then be grouped as needed to define each product. These structures can be simple (only a few levels) to highly complex (many levels deep, containing numerous components and sub-assemblies).

The amount of complexity is a matter of choice in many cases. Your objective should be to strike the right balance that reflects the product design at a sufficient level to manage the production activities efficiently. Structures that are too simple will not provide adequate detail to ensure the right things, in the right places, at the right times. Excessive levels of detail make maintenance and control unnecessarily difficult and costly.

The rationale for deeply complex structures is often rooted in make-to-stock processes, where even components are built to inventory. Another motivation for overly complex structures is the ability to monitor various stages of completion, but modern systems provide many options for easily monitoring the process flow without creating unnecessary BOM levels.

Generally, the objective should be to create structures with levels the mirror the real world conditions. Where do resources go into the processes, and where do things come out that need to be discretely managed? These outputs are either products for sale, or parts and sub-assemblies that need to be built and used as input into the next level of the process.

Structures

From these simple elements, we will be free to create unlimited variations of collections that combine elements into many configurations of products. The structures will map out the relationships between the various elements and show how they will consume resources (costs) when we manufacture them.

The ultimate objective will be to create structures, resulting in products that can be sold for more value than the sum of their parts. This synergistic effect is called profit.

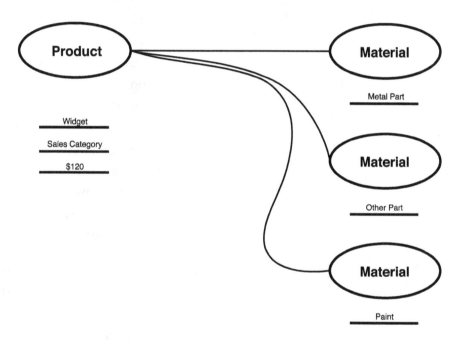

Here is a very simple BOM with just a product and a few materials. Indeed this shows all of the physical parts, but it lacks any description of how they get put together with the activities and costs.

It might seem as though the definition of what constitutes a bill of materials or BOM, should be universally agreed on, but this is not always the case. It all depends on how your company wants to view the data, but my personal favorite is a complete view with all material, activities, and other costs, all organized in one tree structure. This is often called a product structure, as opposed to a BOM.

Next we put it all the elements together into the product structure, combining all the costs of every aspect of the product. This is the complete picture of all the financial attributes, as well as the processes that will combine all of the material elements into our product.

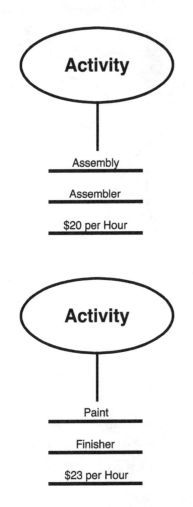

Here we have a couple of activities, which grouped together would typically be called a routing. One advantage to having discrete structures for this purpose, is for convenience and error avoidance in maintaining activities grouped into sets as normal processes, like, the sequence of steps to assemble a category of product. By having the ability to group and recall these routings, building new structures and maintaining existing ones, becomes a bit simpler to manage.

The product structure is one of the most critical data structures in any manufacturing business, and often the one requiring the most attention and cost to maintain. It will drive everything from pricing, to purchasing, to scheduling and work flow patterns. This is the map that reveals the pathways currently used. As such, it is the perfect view for process improvement and cost reduction.

If properly designed, such a structure can also address some other very typical order processing headaches. Ordering the correct product, with all the needed features and options can be slow and fraught with peril. The potential to make a mistake, particularly with complex products, is very large.

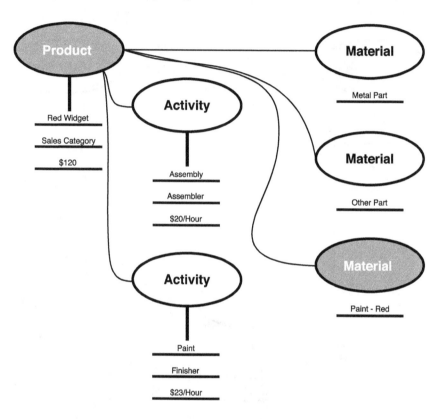

Product Structure for a Red Widget

Here we see our integrated product structure, with all the materials and the activities combined. In this illustration, we chose to highlight one of the materials (the paint), and use the same highlight to code the product. This is the configuration of this product, with the red paint option.

Now with legacy systems we would have to create separate products for each color. That alone increases the possible number of products in our system, and it also makes changes to the BOM's very time consuming and error prone. Imagine a line with just ten colors. Any time any component was changed, ten BOM's would require the identical updates. Any mistake would cause serious problems down the road.

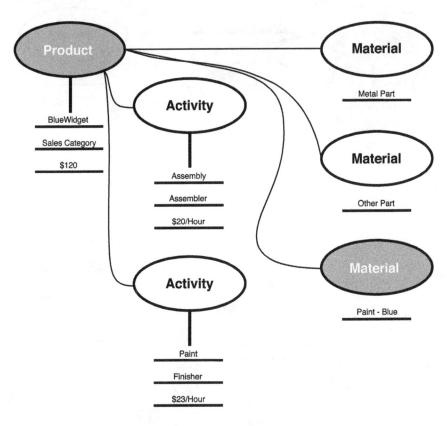

Product Structure for a Blue Widget

Above is a copy of the same BOM, but this time the color material is blue. We can make a BOM for every option of every product, or we can use the structures to build far fewer, configurable or "parametric" products.

With the right kinds of designs, we can build product structures that, rather than fixed with all the options set, can present the user with default values, many of which can be easily changed, possibly by just dropping down a list box. This is also referred to as a parametric BOM, since it is driven by parameters which can be changed by the user, and each one can be programmed with restrictions, and formulae to control the data entry.

Our flexible product structure can now address the issues of changes and much more, opening the door to configurators. A configurator is a template that begins with the product structure for an item. It connects selected input parameters to possible options, all with programmed controls to manage the user input. These options can be something like a dimension, which would cause many components to re-size and re-price. Another type of variable data is a feature from a preset list, such as our color option. Selections in any case can trigger all kinds of calculations, such as up-charges for certain premium selections. The options for control are endless.

When a configurator is used to enter an order, and the selections have been made, then the order is created based on the underlying product structure, populated with all the choices that have been made. This is the ultimate tool to control the entire order process, maximizing speed and accuracy, making the experience as pleasant as possible.

Configurators also open the door to Web commerce, providing the ease-of-use customers are expecting today. Web configurators can be simple parametric entry forms, or they can employ state of the art graphics, showing the customer not only the price, but the exact look based on the selections that have been made.

Configuration of product data can begin with a quotation, or start as a sales order. Your ERP system should segregate these functions and provide tools to manage each type of activity. The data from a quote should also be quickly converted to an order, without the need or the risk of re-entering anything. In a similar manner, production orders can be created to satisfy demand from sales orders.

Simplify

Work orders are the collection of products that will move through the manufacturing process, on a schedule to be completed in response to demand from sales. Based on the product structure of each item, work orders can be for final assemblies, sub-assemblies, components, parts, or whatever you want to call these intermediate steps in the process.

There will often be organization of the shop floor, represented by various work centers, where certain categories of work are done. In some cases the work orders will signify levels in the product structure, where items are completed into a sub-level that will be delivered to a subsequent work center for the next processing steps. For example, a completed sub-assembly produced in work center-A will be consumed in work center-B where the final product is assembled.

Sales Order: SO-001276	
Work Order: 2376-00095	
Pack in Bin	
Testing	
Assembly	

A simple sub-assembly work order, with bar codes to record the activities for costing and tracking.

Templates and Reality

There are two categories of structures, what may be called templates and reality. The former represents a "potential" thing, which has no quantity, and the latter represents the actual item with a quantity. This characteristic applies to elements and collections of elements (structures).

For example, we have a material element, which is defined as 1" x 1/4" NC Machine Bolt., with all the necessary attributes, as we see it in our database. If we buy some of these and put them into inventory, the information from the template is copied to a record, adding that quantity of the item into inventory. In well designed systems, that snapshot of the template is saved with the record of the actual transaction to physical inventory.

Tomorrow the specifications for the 1" x 1/4" Fine Machine Bolt might change. All purchases that follow will be for the new variation, and the incoming inventory must be recognized discretely and distinguishable from the older variation. This may also involve serial or lot tracking, which is an extremely important feature in many industries. Such capabilities are a legal requirement in many kinds of manufacturing and types of products.

So now we can see the distinction between a template for an object and a real world copy, representing a quantity of the item. Taking it a level higher, we can see the same principles at work with the larger structures, this time applying to activities like sales and manufacturing orders.

Using another common example applying typical industry terms, we have a type of template called an engineering BOM, which is how the product is currently designed to be manufactured. This version of the BOM is a template, with the potential for many variations based on choices such as, size, color, certain material options, and so on. So we may actually have a widely varied range of products that can be produced from this one template.

Simplify

With this template previously designed, including the full range of all the features and options connected to it. Every option can have a default value that can be changed, each contributing its cost. We are now ready to process an order.

At that point, the template is opened up much the way a selected Word or Excel template would create a new document, already populated with default values, saving a huge amount to work. That copy of the template is the basis for processing the order. The person entering that order would choose the exact settings for each product from the available options, based on the specifications for the order.

When finished, what is saved to the system is a manufacturing BOM (reality). This record would be a line item on a quotation or some stage of an order, with continued flexibility, allowing for potential changes right up until a work order is created.

When actual production is scheduled, one or more work orders will be created, using the manufacturing BOM that contains all the details for each unique configuration. A line item for quantities greater than one may be grouped together, or split into as many work orders as needed. This will depend on whether serial of lot tracking is involved. Work orders provide a means of breaking up or combining groups of things being manufactured into discrete collections that can be tracked with costs added throughout the process.

It is this template-based, highly variable set of data structures that has allowed us to build product configurators. Configurators may be used in data entry applications on your network, or they may be built into Webpages that can be part of your sales process. They can work for all sales channels from direct consumer, to private customized ordering systems for dealer networks.

Here for example is a simple Website, with a visual configurator allowing the buyer to select shapes, base options, and finishes, and see the results of each choice as a full color 3D rendering, with pricing calculated for each option. These visual configurators currently represent the pinnacle of user interfaces, but just the standardization of all these variables, even using simple non-visual screens with fill-in-the-blank forms, is a valuable result.

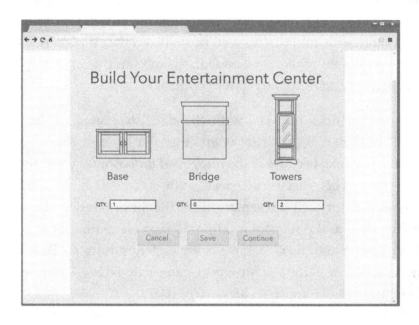

Understanding these design possibilities and where they can lead is very important if your want to guide your company to leverage its investment into every aspect of your business. Knowing the real meaning of the underlying concepts is valuable in setting the right objectives and avoiding backtracking and costly mistakes.

Implementing your new system is a rare chance at a clean start in almost every area. Work simplification opportunities abound as each process is addressed; screens and presentation views defined, reports designed, labels, shop floor documentation, everything is on the table.

While this may all sound somewhat daunting, take it for the positive opportunity that is, one that is not continuous improvement, but a huge leap forward into an integrated world. That integration alone will shave off enormous waste, simply by making more direct connections between data collection and its use.

In the old legacy world of islands, the same information collected once, usually at great cost, must be re-entered from place to place, a costly and error prone methodology. Free of these islands and encumbrances, with your new data grid in place, you will enter information once, and due to well normalized data structures, it will become available wherever needed; reliably and consistently, with controlled access from one point of control.

Simplification does not end with the data structures or the direct benefits of their design. That is just the first layer of return on this investment. Next, because of the improved tools now at your disposal, every place where users interface with data will have simplified access and improved presentation of the information. Improved interface tools and powerful modular design elements, allow screens to be customized to the exact needs for each application. Data that is unnecessary in a particular situation, can easily be hidden from view only in that case, or for that category of user.

These improvements lead to faster access and entry of information, and fewer mistakes or entry errors. Other improvements are also available as the implementation process continues.

Again, due to the power and flexibility you will have with your data grid, every place where data interfaces with your real world, there will be opportunities to make those connections easier, faster, and more reliable. Every transaction where you need data collected, offers the chance to move from manual options to automation, from handwritten numbers to barcodes, from human memory to drop down list boxes.

Implementation of a new information system is a golden opportunity to simplify and cut waste throughout your organization, from the front office to the loading dock.

Strive for Normal

Whether your company is planning to build its own information system or the search is on for the best software package from the available products, knowledge of the structure of the underlying database is critical to the success of your project.

Making a decision based on the look and features of the user interface alone may lead to painful disappointment later when the system is put into service. Promises that the database is fit for your needs should be carefully verified, including answers as to how the database can be modified as future demands are encountered. In fact the user interface is secondary, since a good system should allow users to customize many of the views to their needs.

As we will see, just knowing for example that the database is in a SQL Server is insufficient to judge the quality of the database design. The right database design will meet both current and future needs, since it will have a quality of extendibility, which allows data elements to be added to the structures, without negative impact on the existing data.

In database design, there is the concept of normalization, which helps provide a more solid and reliable foundation for the systems that will access that information for all the activities within your company. This chapter introduces a few of the basics of database normalization, which are well worth taking some time to understand.

When businesses began using computer data storage systems, organization of the "files" was based on the paper documents they would attempt to replace. Also like the paper files, the earliest strategies for data storage made copies of the same information over and over; like the address of a customer being stored in multiple locations throughout the database.

Programmers refer to this kind of data structure as "flat files", since this design tends to represent a very one dimensional view. From a programming perspective, data in flat files requires a lot a work to add, edit, copy, or delete data, leaving all the heaving lifting to the software code. In this world, minor bugs in the software, or unusual, or unpredicted operator actions, can easily cause corruption of the database.

Although many modern software systems still employ some flat file strategies, most actual data storage is in relational databases, which can provide much improved security and access speed. However, just because the data resides in a modern relational database system does not necessarily mean the data is well normalized.

Below is a classic example of data stared in a table that is not normalized. Each row is a record, intended to collect all of the employee skill certifications, where with some employees like George, may have more than one type of certification.

Example of a Flat File Structure:

Employee	Address	Certification
John	Chicago	Electrical
Sam	New York	Plumbing
George	Atlanta	Electrical
George	Atlanta	Plumbing

The problem this design is that the address is repeated with each certification record for George. With two separate records for George, each with an address, it is easy to imagine how the two could get out of synch.

120

In the next example, we see how the data has become out of sync as shown in the same structure with two records for George's skills. When George moved from Atlanta to Macon, only one of the two records was properly updated. This kind of "user error" is very common in such flat file systems. Furthermore, it is also very difficult to spot these errors once changes have taken place, until someone needs that address.

Common Error in a Flat File Structure:

Employee	Address	Certification
John	Chicago	Electrical
Sam	New York	Plumbing
George	Atlanta	Electrical
George	Macon	Plumbing

Here we see that only one of George's two records has been correctly updated, resulting in a data mismatch. Later, how will anyone know which address is correct?

Such an error could easily occur if a worker updated George's address in only one of the two records where it was stored, unaware of the second record. This "flat file" strategy carries extremely high risk and is very labor intensive to maintain.

The better (more normalized) table design is described as follows:

A primary employee table might contain the addresses and other details related to each employee.

Table of Employees & Addresses:

Employee	Address
John	Chicago
Sam	New York
George	Macon

A second table contains a record for each skill certification for each employee. Since there can be more than one certification per employee, this one-to-many organization works well.

Related Table of Skill Certifications:

Key	Certification
John	Electrical
Sam	Plumbing
George	Electrical
George	Plumbing

This second table is joined to the Employee table, using a unique key for each employee record. For illustration, the key is the employee name, but usually it is a hidden value, separate from the actual data.

A Normalized Relational Structure:

Employee	Address		Key	Certification
John	Chicago		John	Electrical
Sam	New York		Sam	Plumbing
George	Macon		George	Electrical
			George	Plumbing

Above we see the one to many relationship that joins the records from the primary employee table to the secondary certifications table. This is an example of one of the foremost measures of normalization; each piece of data is in one and only one location. Only keys are repeated, allowing the key to connect (or point) one record to another. This is an example of what database designers call relationships, which comprise the network of connections between the components of your database.

The user interface that allows access to this data would present only one George, with his address, and because of the relationships, the same view could list George's two certifications. It is a simple task to create such an interface view displaying George's data completely and accurately, without any complicated programming, since the database design does most of the work.

In addition to data integrity, highly normalized data structures will naturally perform better, since their very design reflects the real world they serve. On the other hand, with flat file structures, the programmer must anticipate all of the possible connections between various files and build program routines to manage the resulting "implied relationships". However in a normalized relational database, that programming is essentially built into the data structure.

Another advantage to normalization is speed, particularly if the database is supported on a server system optimized for SQL queries. Such systems can offload a lot of the data processing onto the server using stored procedures (usually queries), triggered by a request from the client interface. The following example contrasts the flat file versus the client/server relational database.

With a flat file or poorly normalized database structure, for example, the user at his computer (the client machine on the network) wants a list of records selected from the database on the server. This could be for a list on his screen or a report that he needs.

In legacy systems, all the possible records (usually the entire table or tables) would be transferred across the network, into memory on the client machine. The software on the client would then sort through all of those records selecting the ones that meet the criteria for the list.

With our well normalized database on a SQL Server type of platform, when the user wants that list, the software sends a special type of message — called a trigger — to the database on the server. On the server the trigger causes the execution of a special type of program — called a stored procedure — that will process the query on the server and return to the client only the records that match the request for the list.

This approach dramatically reduces network traffic since only the query results are sent back to the user, rather than the much larger amount of data that must be transferred if the processing is done on the client machine. This approach is not workable with flat file structures, since the stored procedures operate using SQL queries, which rely on a normalized relational database.

There are many other highly technical terms and methods to normalization, but it is not necessary to get that deep into the jargon to understand the rationale. What is important to understand is the expected results from a well normalized database, so let us dig into just two of the most valuable measures of successful database normalization.

The first has to do with the concept of the data structures reflecting the world they serve. Even as we worked through the issues pertaining to the simple database with worker certification records, we could see how reflecting the real world in our data structure would simplify and reduce the potential risks of errors.

Therefore one of the desired results of normalization is:

Normalized tables, and the relationship between one normalized table and another, mirror real-world concepts and their interrelationships.

Our example provides this result. The table design mirrors these real-world constructs of:

- one employee,

- who lives at an address,

- and has one or more skill certifications

We have structured our data for the best reflection of our real world situation, an important measure of the quality and usefulness of our database design.

Taking this concept to a higher level, specifically addressing the most fundamental construct in nearly any manufacturing environment, we get to the most complete description of a product that we will have in our database. This is the superstructure that embodies every facet of the product, expressed in the clearest terms.

It is often called the product structure, a term introduced in the prior chapter. A product structure typically consists of:

- the bill of materials (BOM) and

- one or more routing structures (activities)

- along with the potential for a multitude of attached files, such as: drawings, documents of all kinds, change orders, etc.

When such complex collections of data are stored and maintained using the legacy flat-file approach, these structures become unstable and quickly hit walls, due to the limits imposed by the one-dimensional organization imposed by these file systems. Add to those limitations the high likelihood that errors will begin to accumulate over time, and we can see more reasons why these legacy structures are unsuitable for today's lean manufacturing demands.

Here again, a graphical view will help highlight these limitations. We will diagram the same product; one in the flat file world with its constraints, and the other in the relational world with the flexibility to map relationships that mirror our real world situation. In preparation for this kind of work, we will want to be sure we fully understand all the process details and how they relate, in addition to all the materials that will be required.

Before we begin, to avoid confusion there should also be a few definitions set out. There are many typical terms used in manufacturing, to represent various stages of the production of a product and its materials; for example, raw material, part, sub-assembly, assembly, final product, and so on.

These terms all imply various stages of manufacture, but they can quickly become ambiguous. Moreover, these terms take on less importance in a make-to-order, lean manufacturing environment, where parts and subassemblies are rarely built for stock.

Therefore, in the following examples we will have only two classes of items in the BOM structure: raw (material) and processed (assembly). The differentiating factor is; does the item contain value from only a single material or have we added anything such as processing labor, other materials, or any other type of cost element?

An example of a raw material is:

Hot rolled steel coil, .05" thick, 30" wide

If we want an item in the BOM that represents this material, cut to a length of 24", then we would normally add at least one labor step, which causes the new item to acquire attributes of time and labor cost and possibly various overhead costs as well.

Most practitioners would call such a processed item a part or component, but again naming the levels of the BOM is not important and in fact can limit design and operational flexibility. These definitions get even more complicated when there are things we can both make or purchase, but we will avoid that complication in this discussion.

Here is where we start to see the importance of first organizing the data into logical elements, and second, grouping them into collections that suit our processing methods and reflect realistic costs. In the above case our collection consists of some coil stock, and an activity to cut it to 24 inches. We probably do not sell this item, so it is just an intermediary step on the way to a product we sell.

Although our first examples for simplicity are focused on just the BOM, it is part of the larger product structure, which also includes routings (collections of activities) and overhead or indirect costs, all totaling to the product cost for one item.

When we add other materials and more labor, we simply increase the complexity of the product structure. The exact organization of this structure is entirely up to your needs, but it should:

"mirror real-world concepts and their interrelationships."

Many BOM structures are also parametric, which mean that some of the components are variable as opposed to fixed values. Attributes such as, sizes, colors, patterns, and even whole sub-assemblies, can be selected as features and options.

In such a system as previously described, the BOM on file is really a template which is used to start the process with certain default values already set, ready for the user to make changes as needed.

These are some of the many benefits that relational structures have over flat file systems. Using a simple flow chart, we can see a graphical representation of each approach, with the same components organized in each of the two ways.

The following two examples contrast the flat and relational structures using a simplified BOM for a bicycle. In the flat structure we find everything on the same level, or in some cases a limited, fixed number of levels, making the data representation out of synch with our real world process. This is an extreme example, but indicative of the limitations such system impose right from the beginning. And as time goes on and products and processing methods change, these limitations hold back potential improvements.

Flat File BOM Structure for a Bicycle:

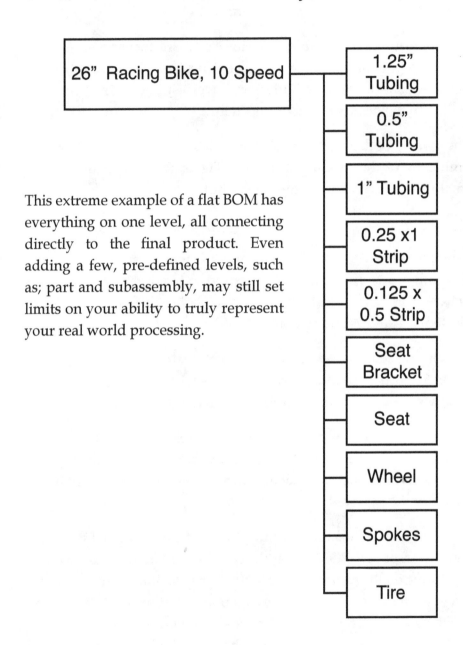

26" Racing Bike, 10 Speed	1.25" Tubing
	0.5" Tubing
	1" Tubing
	0.25 x1 Strip
	0.125 x 0.5 Strip
	Seat Bracket
	Seat
	Wheel
	Spokes
	Tire

This extreme example of a flat BOM has everything on one level, all connecting directly to the final product. Even adding a few, pre-defined levels, such as; part and subassembly, may still set limits on your ability to truly represent your real world processing.

Relational Structure for a Bicycle:

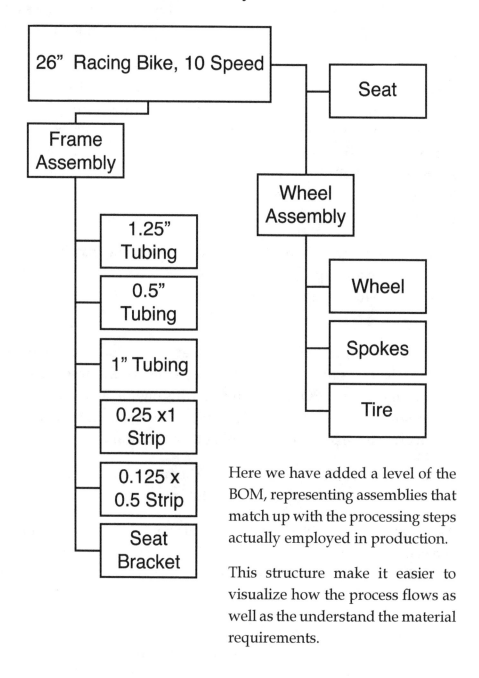

Here we have added a level of the BOM, representing assemblies that match up with the processing steps actually employed in production.

This structure make it easier to visualize how the process flows as well as the understand the material requirements.

These examples begin to reveal the beauty of a fully relational structure. It allows users to mirror the real world, plus it allows for constant change to the structures, facilitated by the modular nature of the components.

One important note here; just because software is built on a relational database system, does not guarantee that the structures are normalized. In fact we have seen many software products built on fully relational database platforms, but the actual table structures are flat, with no relationships at all. This is very common when legacy systems have been ported to a new platform, but the data structures have been kept the same for compatibility, or simply to avoid the effort.

Therefore as a buyer, do not be satisfied just knowing that the system is build on an appropriate foundation like SQL Server or Oracle. It is important to look deeper and make sure the data structures support your needs.

In our flat example, there are only two levels; raw materials and the final product. As previously mentioned, some flat file systems seem to offer multi-level BOM structures, with one or more additional levels, however; they are usually fixed to a specified number of levels, which often have predefined meaning to the software.

While that limitation alone may not seem like a problem, it is a symptom of the data organization that points of future problems in many areas.

As an example of problems caused by this limitation, we next look at one such system composed with pre-defined levels. This particular example is typical of vertical market software for manufacturers that process from sheet stock as a primary raw material.

Envision material that is purchased as sheets, which must first be cut into parts of specific dimensions. Then parts are combined into sub-assemblies and finally products. Many things are made through standardized sequences such as:

130

- Sheet stock is cut to part sizes

- Parts get other processing (boring, grooves)

- Sub-Assemblies are made

- Products are built from parts, sub-assemblies, & other materials

Even in their narrow market category, the legacy system developers failed to imagine what became a large stumbling block. The pre-defined BOM levels were:

- material

- cut part - always made from a single material

- sub-assembly

- product

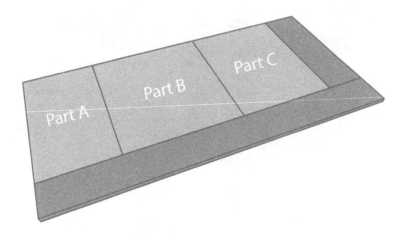

To the designers of our example software system, with only small scale testing, this structure seemed to work. It had material in the form of panels as shown above. These sheets would then be cut into parts, which could go directly into products, or into sub-assemblies.

What other levels could possibly be needed? Soon however, a problem appeared, for which workarounds were of little help.

Not all of the users of this type of system would process panels that were ready for cutting as purchased. Some manufacturers made their own composite panels, which allowed them to sell the exact look any customer wanted, controlling the color and texture of each side, as well as the kind of core that gave strength to the final product.

So instead of buying panels ready for cutting, these companies bought the substrate materials (core) and then glued whatever faces the customer selected, to create custom panels for each project.

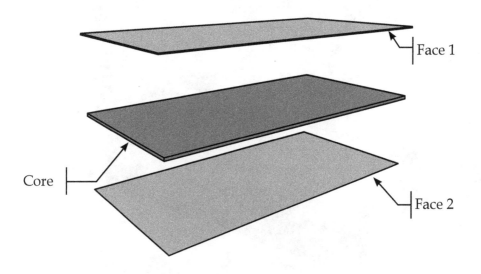

Many decorative materials come in a sheet form. These thin sheets are glued to a thicker core material, often with another face on the opposite side, forming a sandwich type of intermediate component. This sandwich will then be cut to the sizes needed for further processing.

So now we have a type of processed item, which then has to act like a raw material, so that it can be cut into parts. Because of the constraints of the database design, the software is out of synch with the reality of how the actual process works.

Limited BOM Structures - Due to Fixed Levels

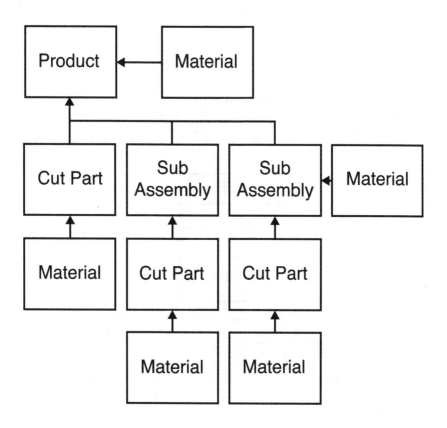

The graphic above shows four fixed BOM levels (only 3 below the parent), with only these possible combinations:

- Cut Parts are only made from Material

- Sub-Assemblies can be made from both

- Products can be made from all

133

Those are all the combinations that are possible given the constraints, however, what we need requires an arrangement that is not allowed by these design limitations.

The designers of this architecture were sure that parts would always be cut directly from materials, or that the difference would never matter to anyone in actual practice. But this kind of built-in constraint has remained a plague of many vertical market manufacturing software applications.

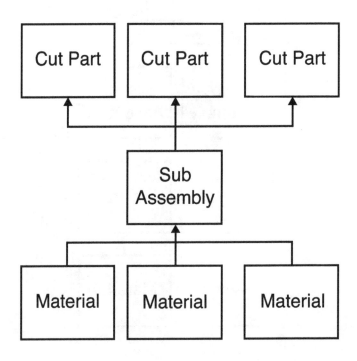

Above is the sub-structure that is needed to solve this problem, using the typical terms. Naming of the levels does not restrict the relationships, so three materials glued together makes the required sub-assembly, which gets cut into parts.

The laminated panel (sub-assembly in the diagram) may then be cut up into the required parts from each sub-assembled sheet. This is the solution that is needed, but the legacy software and its underlying data structures were not designed to allow this level of flexibility.

The legacy system offers only two bad options to work around this constraint.

First option: trick the system, and call this sandwich a material. Then we lose all control over the real materials — the core and the glued on faces — as well as the process to assemble them. We have to create "fake materials" that are really sub-assemblies, one for each combination of laminated panel. This workaround is of course is a maintenance nightmare, but then the fake material could flow though the rest of the standard processing steps, getting cut to size and ready to move on as a part.

Second option: if we did not want to treat this sandwich as a material, then we would have to act as though each individual material would be cut, instead of the glued up sandwich that we really cut. The intermediate parts have no identity as something that could be put on a work order. The mismatch between reality and the data structures requires manual workaround strategies, and lots of additional clerical steps, which still leaves users without the needed controls for good process and materials management.

Either solution is a terrible compromise that causes a great deal of unnecessary work and delay, and is disconnected from the reality of our process. At a glance these problems may not sound like such a big deal, but considering the processing steps that must be scheduled and manually controlled, this type of issue becomes a serious weakness in such a system.

This example is especially realistic since most manufacturers that process these kinds of custom laminations are engineer to order types of companies, therefore many different materials are involved, rather than just a few stock patterns.

This type of faulty design is so seriously flawed that even programming changes to the application cannot overcome the shortcomings. The problem is in the data structure, and sometimes these issues can be so deep that no programming tricks will help.

The appearance of relationships in these types of legacy systems is often only skin deep. When the foundation is a true relational database with well normalized tables, then the relationships between data objects can be changed with simple standard methods.

Legacy systems built on non-relational file structures require the software to create and maintain the logical connections that are lacking in the database itself. In this world of fixed file layouts, there is too much dependency on programming as opposed to the organization of the information. And usually, if the data looks poorly organized, then you might expect that the software is riddled with similar weaknesses.

When there is a need for redefinition of BOM's or process routings, the existing structures may not be able to support it. Be prepared for heavy programming, testing, and transitioning costs. These costs can be so great that resistance to change looks prudent, holding back your company from important improvements, simply because your databases our so out of date.

With proper design, you will have substantial flexibility to define and redefine relationships between the elemental objects representing your business processes. In that way you will have the tools to create an accurate representation of your real world.

In the suggested solution part of our example, we added a logical intermediate item to represent the custom laminated panel as a sub-assembly. Such intermediate processing stages are arbitrary in a flexible BOM structure, and can easily be rearranged as processing changes occur, again synching the data structure with the real world.

Just because an item is in a certain position in the hierarchical structure should not require that it be designated by a particular term, such as subassembly, or cut part. These terms are fine for categorization, but should not constrain the BOM organization, nor should they be allowed to get in the way of proper representation of the actual processes.

It might even make sense describing only two elemental types of BOM items — raw and processed — because, in a way similar to the ambiguity that intelligent numbering may cause, categorizing items by processing stages can also lead to conflicts.

Avoid putting too much meaning on categorizations such as assembly and sub-assembly, or you risk limitations as processing methods change.

One if the problems with our legacy system example, is that the logic is based on false assumptions, because of too much significance put on categories. An assumption was made early in the design of the system, that only raw material was the input for the cutting process. However, in some cases, several raw materials must be combined to create the custom input needed. Since the system put too much meaning on categories, it was impossible to accurately model the real world situation.

In contrast, our next diagram illustrates how reassembling the graphical elements including activities, we can easily depict the true process flow, as we are unconstrained by definitions limiting the order of our building blocks. In the following illustration, the sub-assembly made from three materials is the input for cutting; a true representation of reality.

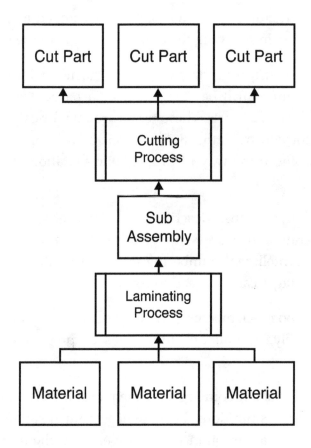

Much more information can now be organized within these kinds of basic structures, simply by adding branches to the trees we have built.

Among the additional elements, we can include all of the processing steps, which when grouped together are usually called routings. Routings themselves carry a great deal of information about process flow and its activities. These routings are components like the materials, which combined with the BOM, describe the entire product structure.

That superstructure defines every cost element in a single product. Here you can start to visualize the product structure as the complete picture, merging BOM, routing, and other costs, for the complete representation of our product.

With a set of these basic elemental building blocks, you can now describe anything you can manufacture from those materials and processing activities. The relational tree that results will graphically represent the cost relationships and dependencies for any product.

You should always strive to define the most elemental components, which accurately represent your materials, activities, and the products that result. These basic elements become the best building blocks for the most reliable data structures, and they are easier to maintain. Good data, well organized and presented, supports the best decisions.

Now that we have explored the rationale behind the importance of normalization in terms of mirroring the real world, let's examine a second important result of the normalization process; the ability to easily expand the data structures to accommodate your changing needs:

When a fully normalized database structure is extended to allow it to accommodate new types of data, the pre-existing aspects of the database structure can remain largely or entirely unchanged. As a result, applications interacting with the database are minimally affected.

This concept is very important for the life expectancy of your system. Requirements will constantly change as your business grows and adapts to new conditions and expectations. The ability to add capacity to store additional kinds of information is very important for a reasonably long overall life-expectancy for your system. Knowing that your data structures will support changes, without painful upgrades and lost time, is insurance that reduces the burdens and constraints on future improvements.

So next let us examine how flat versus relational stands up using the above normalization goal.

Attribute	Value
Product	Widget
Color	Green
Option 1	Extra Battery
Option 2	Blue Stripe

In the above example, we have a fixed structure, with fields for Product, Color, an Option 1 and Option 2. This is fine until we need an Option 3. This is an incredibly common problem that almost everyone has experienced. In some situations, workarounds are possible, but with regard to manufacturing data, these are not satisfactory options.

In such a case, when changes like these are necessary, there is usually a lot of programming and data conversion. These conversion processes can also shut down your system for a while, especially if something goes wrong.

These risks and costs are because these kinds of legacy file restrictions, which make it very difficult to expand data structures in any direction. Changes to the structures become at the very least a complicated, multi-stage process, or even worse, too difficult and costly to afford to make the changes.

Old File

Attribute	Value
Product	Widget
Color	Green
Option 1	Extra Battery
Option 2	Blue Stripe

New File

Attribute	Value
Product	Widget
Color	Green
Option 1	Extra Battery
Option 2	Blue Stripe
Option 3	*new field*

The above diagram illustrates both the old and new record structures for our example. Try to imagine the entire process, just to add this one field to our flat file system:

- The first step in this case would be to create a new empty file, with the additional Option 3 field.

- Then a program would be written to read the first file one record at a time, and copy the fields over to corresponding records in the new file.

- Bad or unexpected values can cause the conversion process to either abort, or worse, just go on and finish as if nothing had happened, leaving unknown errors

- If the copy process works (still with possible errors), then you can modify the data screens that will be used to add and edit the records

- Then finally the users can begin to manually add the Option 3 values to the new file, hopefully finding any conversion errors in the process

This is a time-consuming and costly process even if it succeeds. Once a company has been through this kind of conversion, the costs and problems they encounter may deter them from attempting future changes.

Next we can contrast that process to the relational database world, where our structures should meet the test for expandability. We will start with the relational version of the same green widget, but use a different diagram since the file is now multi-dimensional. In this world, we put the minimum amount of information in each container, and then we connect it to as many other objects as we need. When changes are necessary, we just add more objects and relationship connections.

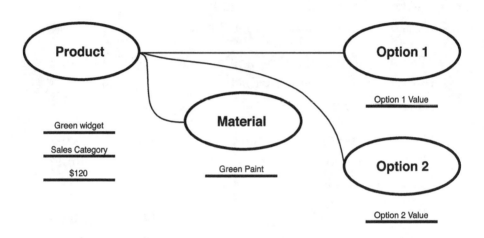

**The same Green Widget
with same fields,
now in a relational structure**

Above is the initial state of the data structure. It represents the same information as the first flat file, but stores that data in a different way. In terms of relational databases, we have a one-to-many relationship, so adding a third option is easy.

Using this object oriented perspective, we can see that it is a simple matter to add one more option object, with its relationship to our product, as below. In fact, we can add as many additional options as needed.

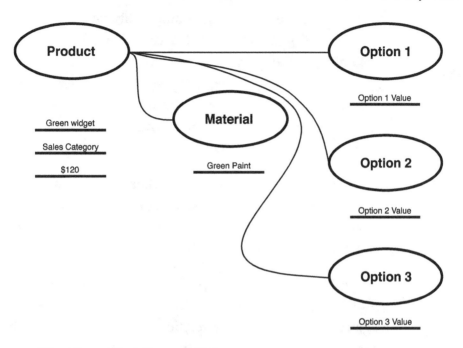

**The Upgraded Green Widget
with Option 3 added
simply by connecting another object**

Most current database management systems will also provide simple tools for the modification of the data tables and relationships. Then the data conversion process, if needed, is often a part of the re-design process, without disturbing the database or any existing connections to any objects.

Here, as with the flat file example, the user interface may need to be modified to add the new attribute. However, that change is much easier in the relational environment, usually just adding a combo box to the screen and connecting it to the new field.

The difference in time, cost, and pain between these two approaches is huge. This type of issue is a major reason that legacy systems remain unchanged through years of suffering, because the modification costs and risks of shut down are simply too high.

Many companies are severely constrained by old or poorly implemented information systems, and a common factor is often the lack of flexibility in the database itself, not just the difficulty in customizing the use interface. Frequently software buyers put too much emphasis on the look and feel of the user interface, when in reality that appearance and superficial functionality is the easiest part to fix.

Adding features on top of a well designed database is simple and predictable. Whereas with a poorly designed or un-connectable data structure, companies are stuck in the mud, unable to make progress without extraordinary expense and difficult workarounds.

Many make-to-order manufacturers provide products offered with a wide range of features and options, which constantly change over time. Here again, the versatility of a relational database provide the foundation for user-friendly functionality, while also ensuring fast and accurate input.

In this world the BOM is a variable object, where there are many options that can be changed for each product on an order. For example, the color many be an unlimited range of possible choices from a specific list of options. Such a structure also makes it a simple matter to create custom interfaces for customers to purchase your products, with each feature and option exactly the way they selected, with far less risk of mistakes. The ability to create and maintain such order configuration interfaces is a huge plus for any system.

Again these relational structures enable these benefits, because it is a simple matter to change the entire tree structure on the fly as the order configuration takes place. Then, once the choices are made, the data is saved in that state, ready for the next steps in the order fulfillment process.

Also your primary information system will never do 100% of the work. It will need to connect to other software and hardware systems. For example, output data to CNC machines, connections to engineering and graphic design tools, Web commerce, output to a payroll data service, and the list will continue to grow. Well designed database systems easily connect to many other types of software, with customization for converting data to and from the proper formats.

The most important point to keep in mind is that your information system is the foundation and connecting network for everything your business does. Envision your database as a plumbing system, managing the flow of vital information, touching every kind of activity throughout your entire business.

We can go on with the plumbing metaphors, such as, leaks representing waste, undersized pipes as constraints limiting the flow, and in fact, those all seem to apply. Thinking in these terms is assisted by the use of graphical tools, like flowcharting, which helps visualize the flow patterns reflecting your real-world activities. Use these tools to work through the design options for your system, and it will be time well spent.

Before building and loading data into a new information system, make sure to carefully consider the design and structure of how that data is organized. Have the major decisions made — what data is needed, and how it should be organized — so your implementation can move forward with confidence. Without a reliable database structure as the foundation, performance, data integrity, security, flexibility, and even usability, will all suffer.

OOP not Oops

Previously, we discussed some very basic but critically important concepts pertaining to the organization of your data. We saw some of the benefits of a normalized database structure, and then noted how the application software would be easier to build and maintain on top of this type of relational design. We even saw how this structure, with its relationships mirroring the real world, in itself would do some of the work previously expected from code.

Now we have the logical foundation to consider the components of your system that capture, manage, and present that information; the software tools that support many activities throughout your business. Like the organization of your data, the applications that connect to it will be better if they too follow similar rules to those governing their structure and behavior, based on elements and collections of basic building blocks.

Let us start with the assumption that you have designed and built a solid foundation structure, on a client server database platform supporting SQL. This is the structure upon which you can build and implement all the software tools used in the business processes throughout your company.

These "applications" provide a means to accumulate customer information, design a new product, process an order, or pay a bill. Within these applications, there may also be a large number of smaller components to manage, address entry, item number selection, and so on. Overall consistency in the look, feel, and functionality of the many user interfaces is an important goal, and these data objects and collections present an opportunity for standardization.

There is a concept in software design and development called Object Oriented Programming (OOP), which simply put, is the opposite of repeatedly reinventing the wheel. OOP seeks to build very useful, well tested, self-contained components (objects) that can be re-used across many applications, with highly predictable results. These objects are much easier to build and maintain than old-style procedural code, and they even allow updated features to be deployed across multiple "instances" of each object. Each instance "inherits" the characteristics of the original object, and can then take on other features.

As with the data structures, this OOP approach applies to all levels from simple bits of code, to complete user interfaces. Reusable components can exist at many levels, and like data structures, they can be nested. In programming, objects "call" each other, which means that one object is using the other for a purpose, such as, converting the graphic of a bar code to ASCII text, or a complete screen object to access an address.

This object oriented approach leads to a much greater degree of consistency from one component to the next, and has the benefit of lower maintenance costs over the long run.

In contrast, most legacy software is built using techniques requiring very large amounts of single-purpose, custom programming even for routine tasks. As a result, across an entire system, the same kinds of components may look and act differently, from one situation to another. Something as simple as the format of an address, may have a different look and feel in various screens, making errors and misunderstandings more likely than if there were greater consistency.

Approaching these issues from an OOP perspective, we would have a single object to contain an address, including all the access methods to add, edit, and delete. That address object would then be used in any situation where it was needed, with totally consistent and predictable results. Users across your entire system would all see the same data presentation, and expect the same input and maintenance methods to work, no matter what application screen they were using.

It is also easy to see how such consistency would be advantageous when viewed from a lean perspective as well. OOP offers the maximum level of flexibility, through the application of interchangeable and reusable objects. This is a necessary attribute in a world of constant improvement. How can important changes be implemented when the barriers and costs are high, as found in inflexible legacy systems?

As with the earlier topics on data design, we do not need to get deep in the technical weeds with OPP or with programming at all. You simply need a high level understanding of the concepts and the how they will benefit your implementation. Being aware and able to recognize these qualities, or lack of, is essential to making the important choices of purchasing and implementing your system.

These concepts are important to keep in mind whether you are building your own information systems, or you are sifting through and vetting the options available on the market. In most cases, companies try to avoid building their own, since these are daunting tasks, with huge learning curves and price tags, and in the case of failure you can only blame yourself.

Most business will instead choose to select a software package, or a solution provider that will customize a package and deliver implementation and training services as well. However, as we have stressed before, choosing to buy does not exempt the buyer from doing the necessary homework.

Caveat emptor — Let the buyer beware!

Our purpose with this chapter and with the others in this book, is to provide the reader with enough information to allow for good decisions. Understanding the meaning and value of these design concepts is key to avoiding the purchase of an inflexible, difficult to customize, and costly to maintain, information system. Software that is built with strong emphasis on OOP methodologies will have a more consistent look and ease of navigation. Training and the learning curve are much more manageable due to a logical and intuitive user interface. Such systems are also easier and less costly to modify or add new features.

So how do we apply this idea of OOP and normalized data, to good interface design or selection of the right software?

- First look for consistency across the user interface. Do the screens employ the same look and feel for similar tasks and presentation of information?

- Does the user have some level of control over the data presentation? A common example is a data grid, where users can drag and drop columns and re-sort the order. These features should work consistently in each view.

- Pay close attention to the methods used to add and update information. Are users asked to do the same things in different ways as they move from one interface to another?

- Can users easily drill down into the data to get at underlying details?

- How much customization is possible without getting deep into the code? Are there any standard tools and methods provided for customization?

- Can order entry be controlled and automated through a definable interface like a configurator for selecting features and options of a product?

- Does the system offer methods for connections to other data sources and applications?

- Is it possible to automate receiving and sending these kinds of data, using standardized and predictable methods?

These a few measures of flexibility that are easy to spot if you know to look for them. These features are tell-tale signs, seen right near the surface, without digging into computer code. It is not necessary to have a deep knowledge of programming to see such clear indicators of the quality of the system design and architecture.

Beware of the software demo that fails to address these issues of sound design of the data structures and flexibly of the user interface. Put the highest priority on the underlying structures and the system's flexibility and customization potential of the user interface. The details can then be adjusted to your exact specifications.

It is not necessary that every aspect of the interface is perfect for your needs, and in fact when that is the case, you are probably working with a very narrowly defined vertical market product, which is not the best option in most cases. However, it is critical that you will be able to make modifications at many levels throughout the system, to meet your specifications today and the keep ahead of the constant changes required over time, as your business adapts to the dynamics of your market.

What follows from this basic discussion of data and programming concepts, is the practical application of it all. We will transition into some topics that address designing and implementing your system in such a way as to ensure your data is kept in good condition—the "keep it clean" part of the 5S methodology.

Then we jump right into the whole implementation process, making decisions about how to build the actual data that will form the foundation of every business process, from quotations to accounting.

As you get further along the implementation road, you will collect and maintain large amounts of data. This process will be shared among users of all kinds, each requiring their own perspective to complete their work efficiently. As this complexity increases, you will see the huge benefits from taking the time to understand these logical concepts, and from applying them to your data management.

The solidity, reliability, and flexibility resulting from all this care and preparation, will prove their worth.

Keep It Clean

The moment an information system has been put into operation, the work of keeping it clean begins. Just like production machinery, information systems need constant maintenance to ensure top performance and reliability.

This is obviously true with regard to the hardware that supports your system; the servers, desktops, notebooks, and all the other physical devices. They all need periodic updates to operating systems, drivers, and so forth. However, we are now concerned about your precious data, not just the equipment or the software.

Everyone knows it is a best practice to backup your data, and have redundant strategies for doing so. Our focus in this chapter is on keeping that data clean; free of corrupted records, duplicates, incorrect entries, and data loss. One of the primary sources of this kind of contamination can be the users who enter and maintain your data. This is a particularly difficult task to manage when many people have access to the database.

Here again the first line of defense against these potential problems is the database design itself. As we have previously seen, good design of the database can prevent certain types of errors commonly found due to poorly structured file systems. The proper structure will greatly reduce the likelihood of many common entry errors on the front end, as well as make maintenance simpler and performance faster.

As with other well managed business activities, data entry must have logical rules and procedures governing the work. Well designed interfaces for input and maintenance will go a long way toward helping ensure the procedures are followed. The layout and automation features of data entry forms should be consistent and logical. Wherever possible, common elements should be used for similar types of data.

This model building can be custom configured in many ways

All of these features and options can be selected

The ultimate type of controlled entry form is a configurator. Here everything comes together; the relational design, convenience and simplicity of object oriented programming, all ensuring the fastest and most understandable data entry process. The example above shows how well many features and options can be presented to the user, making the selection process clean and error free.

Organization of these design elements should follow the same formatting conventions throughout your system, so users will become accustomed to the placement of typical entry variables. Standards for the display and presentation of the variables should be established and maintained to reduce the possibility of misreading or misunderstanding the information.

At all times, redundant entry should be avoided. Let the software manage lookups and data validation. Let it find duplicates and warn of possible errors rather than burdening the worker with unnecessary opportunities to enter data elements incorrectly.

Sales Order: SO-001276	‖ ‖‖‖ ‖‖‖ ‖‖‖ ‖‖‖ ‖‖‖ ‖‖
Work Order: 2376-00095	
Cut	‖ ‖‖‖ ‖‖‖ ‖‖ ‖‖‖ ‖‖‖ ‖‖
Laminate	‖ ‖‖‖ ‖‖‖ ‖‖ ‖‖‖ ‖‖‖ ‖‖

Automated entry using bar code scanners and other technologies is a another great way to avoid input errors as well as reduce labor costs and processing time. Many types of transactions can be processed by scanning one code, which is the key that triggers multiple transactions.

For example, scanning a bar code on a work order at a particular work center, causes several material transactions, back-flushing predefined materials from the BOM into the cost of production. This kind of data collection will be examined in more detail in the next chapter.

In addition to all of those transaction details, our main goal is to collect data that helps manage and monitor each process, with the minimum of effort or intrusion on the work. As a result, we can easily present status information about the progress of any work order on the shop floor.

WO#	Item	Qty.	WC: Lam	WC: Cut
2376-00094	Wht Panel	23	23	23
2376-00095	Red Panel	50	50	20
2376-00096	Blue Panel	30	0	0
2376-00097	Pink Panel	87	0	0

50 pieces scanned thru lamination   20 pieces scanned thru cutting

Here for example is a presentation of orders that show panels going through a laminating and cutting process. One simple grid indicates the quantities that have gone through the two work centers, making it easy for managers to see the complete picture at a glance.

At the same time, transactions recording the costs of activities at this work center should also be processed, indicating completion of these parts through the work order. That information feeds into the next process since now we know the components we need are complete and ready as input for the next steps. The point of all this simplified data entry and process integration, is that it greatly reduces the opportunities for errors at the same time as we efficiently collect critical metrics to measure the output.

These kinds of simplification can have a great impact on the quality and quantity of data collected. In the above example, numerous details were accurately collected with each scan. We have integrated a number of steps into one batch process, reducing costs and improving the quality of data collection.

Another tool in common use today is the touch screen, which eliminates the need for typing input data. Touch screen monitors can be located at key positions on the shop floor, at shipping and receiving docks, or any place where transactions need to be collected quickly and accurately. They will feature big buttons, with quick access to the items needed, so that workers can select the work order or other information with a simple touch of the screen.

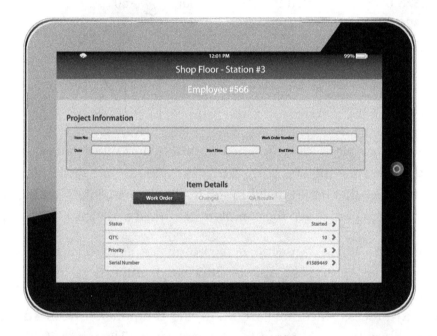

With the increasing popularity and low cost of tablet computers, touch screen input can be at any location where a WIFI connection is available. Even smartphones can be equipped with custom applications allowing field crews to collect data remotely.

These input methods eliminate manual entry which is the most common source of input errors. Typing takes time and skill, plus it requires users to accurately enter data that they may not know how to spell correctly. What happens to those typos? They are all accumulating in your database, messing it up and potentially generating errors that will eventually need to be corrected at great expense.

Often one of the keys to collecting and maintaining clean data is the simplicity of the process. The right combination of technology, planning, and logical design will lead to quick and clean data processing activities, which can also yield the necessary information in the least intrusive way. Careful design with consistent and well organized layout will help keep your data clean and healthy.

Fortunately, the user interfaces and input systems are all just the covering over your database. These components should be easily customizable for both the initial implementation and to accommodate the ongoing changes that your dynamic business will require.

See the Forest And the Trees

One day during a visit to a manufacturing company in Ohio, we ended up in the production manager's office. One end of his desk, along with a large part of a nearby credenza, was covered with stacks of time cards. These were the type that were filled out by hand, collecting not just clock in and clock out times, but also job numbers, operations, and quantities.

Those of us who have been around manufacturing plants have often seen time cards like these. When I asked how this information was used, the manager replied that most of the details were not used at all. They had no way to accumulate and present the information for analysis, other than by costly and time consuming, manual methods.

Although the original objective had been to collect job cost data on top of time card entries, they were not capable of inputting and managing the other information. Therefore, by the manager's own admission, the shop workers were expected to take the time to comply, while management failed to even look at the details, let alone make any decisions based on all this expensive but useless data.

The workers, following instructions from management, were spending precious production time recording detailed statistics that would never be used. For that size operation, such mandated waste multiplied by their large workforce, amounted to a huge number of lost production hours, resulting in thousands of dollars per month spent for nothing. And of course each of these workers had that much less time to devote to actually building the company's products.

This practice is much more prevalent than would be expected. Although in many cases the waste is much less pronounced than in this example, such practices are everywhere. In fact it is only one type of data mismanagement that serves no useful purpose.

When we also consider the number of unused reports and other wasteful activities commonly practiced in this manner, it is easy to imagine large numbers of cost and time saving opportunities, simply by eliminating these unnecessary activities.

Of course, each of these examples started out with a good purpose. Management initially had no intention of wasting time or money. Their purpose was to collect important data that would help improve productivity, not hinder the process. No one plans for this kind of waste, but it can easily happen when the full impact of such decisions becomes clear.

In this particular example of direct labor time collection, there is also a common fallacy at work. Even if the workers are diligent in recording the information, this type of record keeping is highly error prone. The worker's priority should be on productivity; manufacturing a quality product, using the minimum processing time. The paper time card entry runs counter to those goals, therefore something will suffer.

For those of us that have seen these time cards in practice, we know the quality of the collected data is often very low. In fact, shops that pay from these cards will usually admit that errors are rampant. Typically this means that someone from accounting will spend significant time questioning workers and supervisors each pay period, just to get the hours to total correctly. And if the other details are checked at all, we often find that they make no sense.

Name:	John Smith
Clock No:	15793

Start	Activity	WO	Quantity
7:00	Laminate	93-1297	20
8:45	Cut	"	20
9:10	Laminate	93-1299	45
10:35	Cut	"	45

For example, just one aspect affecting the accuracy of this type of time reporting:

- The worker records the time he has begun processing job A, which begins the clock ticking.

- With the primary pressure on productivity, he may forget to clock out of job A when processing of parts for job B begins.

- Then later when the worker finally remembers, and "clocks out" of job A, he has already been on job B for some time.

- At the end of the day, do these statistics have any value?

Worse, we find that many apathetic workers will conclude that this whole process is a waste of effort. They choose to wait until the end of the day, and then fill out the card from memory, making sure that the total hours are correct, but caring little about the incremental times for each individual production job. They are deliberately recording useless data, because they know it will never be checked. Their only concern is getting paid for the correct number of hours.

Of course there are also many other potential errors regarding this type of manual data collection. The job number, product, or even the quantity produced are typical mistakes that may be recorded.

This manual time card example is just one typical situation, out of many common wasteful data collection practices. In most cases, these practices were begun for seemingly good reasons, but the consequences were not considered prior to implementation.

Most companies have many such wasteful processes, most of which started out well meaning, but for one reason or another transitioned into underutilization or even complete disuse. How many reports are routinely run that no one actually reads?

What about those required data fields that must be filled in time after time, however in practice result in useless information being collected for no purpose? Something as simple as a categorization code, which started out meaning something, but in time turns out to be of no real value. These small bits of information can add up to a large amount of wasted effort, as well as a great deal of data that adds no value.

The worst of these examples are the data that users input which is known to be wrong from the start. These are small details that became required to complete a form, to enter an order or setup a new customer. The worker must fill in the blank with something, but may not really know the correct answer, or knows that the data will never be put to use anyway. Workers become apathetic when they come to believe something they are expected to do, is meaningless. As a result, deliberately incorrect data is collected and is now part of your database.

These kinds of problems will gradually seep into any complex system. Again, while people do not usually set out to collect useless information, over time it will happen.

Although the paper documents in our example are usually referred to as time cards, they are really management's attempt at collecting job cost data, with a focus on labor dollars from each worker. However this micromanaging of worker time, particularly for activities that vary widely, based on order details, is of little value even when the data is collected accurately. Processes and methods are often changing in dynamic lean environments. Even without that sort of change, the products themselves are often substantially variable. Often workers join in teams of two or more, working together on the same work order or collections of orders.

So is it futile to even try to collect detailed statistics about the production process?

After World War II during the rebuilding process in Japan, the military command wanted census data. General Douglas MacArthur enlisted the help of William Edwards Deming, an American professor of statistics, author, and business consultant. While in Japan Deming also lectured on statistical quality control, to packed audiences of Japanese business leaders and engineers, influencing the founders of companies like Sony and Toyota.

Deming was invited as a consultant to the Japanese auto industry, and his statistical quality control ideas were widely adopted. At that time, Ford was buying transmissions from one of those Japanese plants, and discovered a troubling result. US customers favored the models with the Japanese transmissions, because they lasted longer. Both the American made and the Japanese transmissions were built to exactly the same specifications, so what was going on?

Ford engineers took some of those transmissions apart and measured every critical dimension. Each part was significantly better than the required tolerances. It was as if the specification called for plus or minus 1/8" the Japanese would build it to within 1/16" every time. They were building the products better than the minimum specifications, something the Ford engineers found baffling. However the tight controls that the Japanese manufacturers were using not only improved the tolerances, but they were also the source of significantly improved overall productivity in the plant. With fewer problems along the production line, throughput was smoother and at higher rates.

In Japan, they quickly came to understand the importance of measuring and controlling these critical details, and the return on that investment came in many ways; better productivity, fewer repairs, greater reliability, higher perceived value. This thinking formed a key component of the strategy for the Japanese takeover of the top position in the auto industry.

Deming advocated that all managers need to have what he called a System of Profound Knowledge, consisting of four parts:

1. *Appreciation of a system:* understanding the overall processes involving suppliers, producers, and customers;

2. *Knowledge of variation:* the range and causes of variation in quality;

3. *Theory of knowledge:* the concepts explaining knowledge and the limits of what can be known.

4. *Knowledge of psychology:* concepts of human nature.

The first two parts of Deming's system, are far simpler to apply today than during the 1950"s, when most statistics were manually collected and tabulated on paper. Today we have an abundance of low cost computing power and advanced data collection tools.

Part one on Deming's list, is critical for improvements of any kind. Without a good understanding of these processes, how can weaknesses be seen? How can bottlenecks be found, or redundancies come to light? Mapping out the business processes is a great starting point for learning what things to measure.

Part two involves the data collection and analysis, which provides the metrics for corrections. These data highlight not just where the problems exist, but also the magnitude of the variation from your target, which is essential for prioritization of each of the issues. It is important to note that in most cases, the data collected measures quality and throughput, rather than individual worker time.

Part three relates to ideas we have discussed about differentiating between useful knowledge and concepts that are simply accepted as common sense that may not apply in every case. Especially in rapidly changing technologies, constant reassessment of the state of the art is important just to keep from falling behind.

And part four relates to the realization that human nature will play a strong role in the success or failure in implementation of new concepts. We have seen how people can easily work against the flow, and still feel that they are actually looking out for the best interests of the company.

Seeing the forest and the trees is about collecting and managing the right data in the least intrusive and most cost effective manner. We have seen an example of how not to collect information, now let us look at some options for more efficient methods.

There are many ways to collect the critical information about your business processes. The best approaches will result in the minimum of interference with the process itself. Contrary to the paper time sheet example, integration of data collection with other aspects of the process is often possible.

As always, the best solution begins with carefully stating the objectives. In our time card example, the company started out trying to collect job cost information. If only payroll was the issue, a simple time clock at the door would work fine, and in fact that is usually the case anyway, since accuracy is legally, as well as financially important.

Here are some metrics that apply well when our main objectives are quality and throughput (highest volume at lowest cost):

- Primary goal: measure throughput

- Account for materials, other costs

- Attribute productivity to each work center

- Accumulate job cost by work order

The paper time card failed to meet the most basic needs, even though it is supposed to be about job cost, it really is just a poor time card. That being the case, such an approach usually fails to collect meaningful job cost.

Our new approach is centered on the productivity of the work center, not any one particular employee. It will accurately measure throughput in units per time, and it will trigger other costs to be added to the work order cost, which are attributable to those activities at that work center.

In collecting the information we need, we will strive to synchronize our data capture with the actual process flow. Additionally, each processing step may trigger one or more data transactions. How difficult is that?

For example, a process step that is collected using a bar code, will of course count the number of products, however that counting can also allocate labor from that work center, to the associated work order. In fact, each scan can easily trigger a number of pre-defined transactions, affecting inventory and overhead, as well as direct and indirect labor.

The above two-step scan document, allows a great deal of information to be collected, quickly and with no written or typed entry. This kind of data collection process does multiple things with little effort, while keeping costs low and with minimal interference with the work.

This is still another synergistic effect, made possible by a combination of data capture hardware and a well designed database system. Bar coded documents like these can be labels, or paper travelers; whatever you call them, they can be extremely powerful tools, not just to capture all this data, but also serve as simple, easy to read work order information, to identify items and track the process flow.

Next, we will revisit our previous process flow chart, this time examining how the details of many associated transactions can be quickly and accurately collected. Automated data collection eliminates inaccurate and time consuming manual entry.

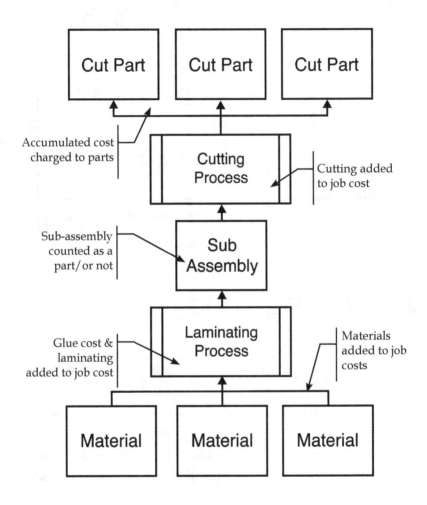

Everything in the above example will be measured accurately and at the appropriate point in the process where the cost is accrued, all using that one simple to use, two-step bar coded traveler.

We can also use more bar codes as needed to simplify flow tracking over a wide range of applications.

Sales Order: SO-001276	
Work Order: 2376-00095	‖ ‖‖‖ ‖‖‖‖ ‖‖‖ ‖‖‖‖ ‖‖‖‖ ‖‖‖
Shipment	‖‖‖‖ ‖‖‖‖ ‖‖‖‖ ‖‖‖‖ ‖‖‖ ‖‖
Final Pack	‖‖‖‖‖ ‖‖‖‖ ‖‖‖‖ ‖‖‖‖ ‖‖‖‖ ‖‖
Pre Pack	‖‖‖‖‖ ‖‖‖‖ ‖‖‖‖ ‖‖‖‖ ‖‖‖ ‖‖
Testing	‖‖‖‖‖ ‖‖‖‖ ‖‖‖‖ ‖‖‖‖ ‖‖‖‖ ‖
Assembly	‖‖‖‖‖ ‖‖‖‖ ‖‖‖‖ ‖‖‖‖ ‖‖‖ ‖‖

The above document is another example of a "traveler", which in this case is for a final product, going through a series of production processes. It represents a simple sequence of processing steps, which in this case would assemble and ship one final product. Travelers may represent individual items (serial numbered if needed) or production "lots", generally more than one of the same item.

In this case the steps from assembly to shipment are shown in reverse order, but that is just a presentation choice. Next to each step of the process there is a bar code, which can be scanned when the product completes that step — very simple.

For our example, let us assume one or more workers at that point in the process, usually a work center. It is a simple matter for the software to calculate the labor hours and cost, on a per part basis, as the parts are counted. Doing so eliminates the need for the worker to record his time to any part or project. This "two for the price of one" measuring is a great way to reduce the burden on the process, while at the same time collecting a lot of useful information.

And what was recorded in our database as each scan in each work center took place?

1) Assembly
   a) counts the item complete through WC
   b) back-flushes BOM items to job cost
   c) time/part in WC (labor, machine, utilities)
   d) adds OH and other factors to job cost
2) Testing
   a) counts the item complete through WC
   b) back-flushes BOM items to job cost
   c) time/part in WC (labor, machine, utilities)
   d) adds OH and other factors to job cost
3) and so on...

All of these important actions for each processing step, are collected with one scan for each stage of production, where the multiple transactions are all triggered by the same event; completion of the product through a measured work center. So, with a few non-intrusive, low-cost scans, the worker quickly and accurately collects all the needed information, including how many products per hour he or his crew made.

Time and again it has been proven that good measurements are necessary and valuable management tools. We have also seen that simply collecting data can be a huge waste, if that information cannot be put to good use.

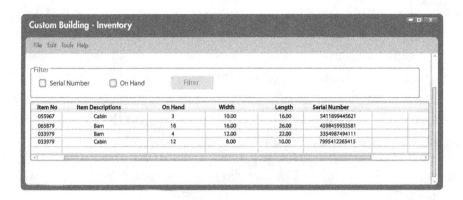

The key concept is striking a balance, collecting what is necessary information, and using methods that impose the minimal interference to the process.

To accomplish these results, you lean on your well designed database, with structures that mirror your real world, allowing you to manage and collect accurate metrics about all of your processes.

Once you have good data collection methods operating as you need, then presentation of the results is the final step. You do not want to waste the collection effort by failing to use the precious information you have worked so hard to accumulate.

From that foundation, you can build the best collection and presentation tools to address your current needs. To design the best methods requires deep understanding of the processes, and good knowledge of the tools available to address the data collection at the lowest possible cost.

The output side of your information system can come in many forms, from reports, to queries presented on screen, and including dashboards that incorporate multiple data views simultaneously.

Printed reports are among the worst output tools, since they quickly age and often fall into disuse. We have all seen the stacks of standard reports on managers desks, knowing that very little of that paper will ever be put to good use. However there are certainly many cases where printed documents are necessary, as demonstrated by multi-purpose travelers used to collect shop floor data.

Often a better presentation solution is an on screen grid, organizing the needed information in rows and columns. Systems today will include many such presentation tools that allow users to filter, sort, and organize their data, using simple methods that let any manager become adept at finding the information he needs quickly. In many systems, views such as these are easily saved, if the user expects to need that presentation in the future.

These types of presentation tools should be on your "must have" list. Without control over the views, your valuable information is difficult to use.

Here we see a grid presenting inventory data, meeting the criteria specified in a lookup. The manager can quickly organize the information as needed, displaying only those records that are required, and eliminating the unnecessary clutter of records that are not needed.

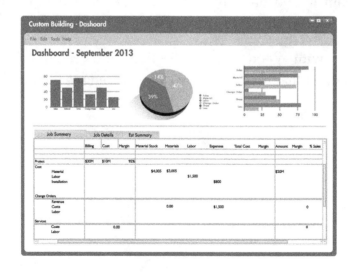

A Wide Range of Project Data Concisely Presented in this Custom Dashboard

Above is an example of custom presentation called a dashboard, which displays multiple kinds of data in one concise view. The individual elements in this dashboard all contain real-time data, queried from the database based on the exact criteria the user specifies.

Tabs along the top of the grid even allow the user to select different categories of details for display. This is just one of an infinite range of possibilities available with the software and database tools found in a modern ERP system.

Real-time presentations on a computer or other device makes your data much more informative and your control over processes more dynamic. Whatever the output medium, it is important that the information is presented in a format that is quickly understandable and filters out unnecessary clutter. Each presentation view should be as simple as possible to minimize confusion and bring the main elements into perspective at a glance.

With the tools offered by a modern normalized, relational database, and quality interface components available for presentation, we can easily zoom in and out, diving into the details where needed, and otherwise getting the treetop view for big picture.

Therefore, with good data collection and carefully designed presentation of that information, we can indeed see both;

...the forest and the trees.

Order Pizza

Other than a startup company, it is rare that the time required to implement a new system is available during the normal course of business. If you were not busy in the first place, you probably would not be in a position to invest in a major new software system. Almost by definition, your company is very busy and the workload is growing.

So then how does the implementation get completed in a reasonable time frame? There will be setup of new hardware, installation of software on servers and connected computers, cleaning organizing and importing old data, new data setup and entry, training — the list goes on. There are just so many details, so many things to plan, so much work to get everything setup...

One my personal favorites of the many quotations attributed to Thomas Edison:

> *"Invention is 1% inspiration and 99% perspiration."*

The same thing can be said of any worthwhile achievement, including many of the things that were done to build your company in the first place. Your team needs to understand that the wonderful results they all want, are only going to happen through dedication, focus, and hard work, just like their other hard-won achievements. Success will not come simply by making the correct choices. Somewhere along the line, the hard work of executing the plan will come into play. In my experience, that is when you order pizza!

Nothing happens without a commitment, which means put it on the calendar, and allot sufficient resources to complete the work. It is quite common for companies to invest in information systems, only to fall behind planned implementation targets very quickly. The typical rationalization for such failure is that there was insufficient time to work on the new system due to the heavy workload needed to keep up with normal business. Such thinking seems to imply that somehow the overload situation had not been anticipated in the first place; a conclusion good managers should try to avoid.

Of course the normal workload was well known prior to the start of the new implementation, and it was also known that the new system would require considerable effort, however, this is one of those conundrums where the pain relief seems too far off into the future, so the cure is not taken and procrastination sets in. Like any rehabilitation, it takes extra effort and even more willpower and endurance, but the results are worth the additional short term burden.

What do most companies do if they land that huge new opportunity which requires more hours than the normal workday? If the schedule is already quite full, do they pass up the big sale? No! They put in some overtime!

If your company had just purchased an expensive new piece of equipment, which had been delivered and installed, but remained unused because the operators lacked training, or because the tooling needed had not yet been purchased, would this result be acceptable? Someone might even be fired if that investment failed to produce the expected returns on a timely basis. However, software systems continue to be viewed in a completely different light than almost any other type of investment.

Decisions leading up to a purchase, requiring commitments of resources, should be made on the basis of typical return on investment calculations. Buying and implementing software should be bound by the same good business logic governing any other expenditure. As such, the implementation process must be planned and managed with the same focus and resolve that would be applied when setting up new machinery, or accepting a large production commitment that presses capacity. It takes a commitment to timetables and the necessary resources to successfully complete the project.

One ERP implementation, where my team was responsible for a large part of the setup, had to be completed in a very short amount of time. No major disruption to normal operations could be tolerated either. We had to find a way to keep up with the normal flow of business, and at the same time, transition into a complete ERP system, replacing every other system currently in use.

The solution was to keep the majority of the team working mainly on the existing systems during normal working hours. Then in scheduled after hours sessions comprised of highly focused teams, we would do the planning and initial decision making for the new ERP system.

This approach removed the pressure of normal activity and interruptions, allowing everyone to become far more focused on the work at hand. Given the breadth of experience of our team, and the unusual focus we all had in these afterhours sessions, the output was very high. We ate a lot of pizza, but met our goals for each go-live component of the system.

These evening sessions allowed us to do the kinds of work that required substantial decision making, with all of the interests of each discipline represented. We had management staff from every area so that all the information and experience would be available, with few reasons for delay.

There were no excuses, and everyone was well motivated to get each task completed well and on schedule. At the same time, everyone knew that if our time was used efficiently and we were productive, the extra work sessions could be reduced and finally eliminated, which in itself provided some extra motivation to our team.

There are many categories of work that teams such as these can complete in these kinds of afterhours sessions, such as:

- decisions about changes to data conventions, like item numbering and BOM organization

- data definitions for activities and work centers, based on the new features and options

- chart-of-accounts designations for transactions

- structure and organization of data, categories, etc.

- decisions on data conversion strategies

- when to convert old data versus when to start fresh

- planning work assignments for data entry (usually work day activities)

These are all things that managers and supervisors can do to get a jump on the activities that might otherwise delay normal implementation work. It is very common for data entry work to get delayed simply because a question regarding naming or categorization had not yet been decided by management.

Anticipate the need for these decisions and make them well before they can become work stoppers when data needs to be entered to meet a schedule. These kinds of decisions cannot be delegated, so make them a high priority, and set aside the time to complete this work thoroughly.

Because this kind of extra-curricular work schedule can be grueling to everyone involved, there is plenty of incentive to get the job done expeditiously, without even considering the ultimate benefits of the fully functioning system.

This is just another reason why the projected benefits should be well articulated and thoroughly understood, so that every member of the team is convinced that their hard work is leading to substantial improvements. This buy-in is essential to keeping the team pulling in the same direction, and putting in the extra effort.

As the project develops, it will naturally transition from planning to actual use. The result will shift the workload more to regular daytime hours as the team begins training and testing on the system. Transitioning in this gradual way reduces the stress and allows for a more cushioned acclimation of the users to the new environment.

Team spirit and buy-in should be the result of all the due diligence that went into the decision in the first place. All of those questions, all of the debate over features and options, all of the claimed benefits with their expected costs and returns calculated... These were the steps taken earlier, which also convinced everyone involved that this is all worthwhile, and now the validation process confirming those choices is in full swing.

It takes that kind of commitment to make these major improvements, but it is always worth the effort, and if done well, the extra hours needed will fall back to normal very quickly. As components of your new system come online, pressure begins to subside, the relief can be felt, the pain is being eliminated.

Of course there are always hired guns; third-party specialists to provide technical assistance with setup, implementation, customization and so forth. These types of resources should be taken advantage of where suitable, and in many cases will be necessary. There are definitely tasks that experienced contractors can complete faster and more cost effectively than would be expected from your busy staff. However, contractors, consultants, and other specialists are not a substitute for the planning, management, and full participation of your team.

No outsider can take ownership of the implementation as well as your team can. They have been the ones feeling the pain and they want to feel the relief that this effort will ultimately bring. It is your company's improvement project, and only through commitment and dedication will your goals be achieved.

DIY

What kind of title is this? Do it yourself? Yes, but that is not to say go it alone. What do-it-yourselfer does not have at least one shelf full of how-to books? Part of the very nature of the concept is that the doer is capable of learning by self study. However, it is very common for management to avoid this responsibility by contracting out the decisions.

In fact, when it comes to just selecting an ERP system, many companies will hire consulting firms to manage the process. Beware, there is no substitute for doing your own homework.

We have talked about the importance of ownership, and that starts with owning the objectives of the project. Hiring out the selection and implementation to an outside vendor does little to guarantee success. It supposedly solves the software selection process, but how do you know you have selected the right consultant in the first place? Was a problem really solved, or did you simply add another layer of cost and administration to the project?

Although they will all claim to the contrary, consultants usually have their own agenda, which like your company, involves making as much money from each opportunity as possible. In the worst case, they will also try to guide your management toward purchasing a specific brand, with the potential for compensation of some sort from that vendor. All of this runs against your best interests, adding costs, with a good potential for a bad final result.

DIY

However, even experts know when to call in help for guidance and assistance in exceptional situations, or where the cost of the tools for the job would be too high for a one-time use. There is nothing wrong with investing in the guidance and support services that specialists can provide. But without question, the planning and decision making should be done in house by your management.

Nor does a DIY approach equate to building everything from scratch, but of course that is a option. Some companies choose to build their own systems from the ground up, but that is not what we mean by DIY. Building systems from scratch requires large resources and very specialized expertise. It will usually take a lot longer, and in fact never ends. Once you start down that road, be prepared to keep the checkbook open as the costs will likely grow beyond the estimates. And your internal programming staff may well become the prima donnas, holding the keys to your new system.

The better answer is to recognize that given there is no totally standard solution, the best starting point is selection of a strong platform for building your dream system. Through the implementation process, everything can be adjusted to your current and future needs. With a strong foundation of a well designed database, and software with the flexibility to allow customization of the interface, reports, and presentation views, your team can plan and implement the customization which will provide the perfect blend.

Even assuming that your company has carefully selected and purchased an ERP system, complete with the full range of modules that address all of your needs — as well as services to help get up and running — there will still be a great deal of the implementation process that falls squarely on the system owners. And you would not want it any other way.

Take ownership. This is the number one factor behind success or failure of any major change. This ownership mindset must begin at the top. Management from the top down must be willing to own the process, not simply make the decisions and write the checks. Some of the most common failures for example, start with the VP Finance, getting the order from his CEO to buy a new ERP system. Where is the rest of the management team on this?

Once a choice has been made, the first category of work to be done is the overall strategic plan for the implementation. There will be many options as to the sequencing of module installation and setup for example. There will be many decisions and numerous kinds of startup work to get your system implementation rolling. Your company knows its needs and available resources better than anyone, so again, these kinds of decisions and implementation planning should be handled internally.

One of the first components of your plan will be assignment of people to the appropriate tasks that will be needed. As discussed in the previous chapter, there are ways to squeeze out some planning time, but first you must decide who is on the team and what role each person will play.

Now let us consider the traits of the team members. There will probably be a wide range among the candidates, with differing levels of skills and experience. On the one hand, we value the education and experience among our most seasoned team members. Many have years of practical knowledge accrued from their education and work experience, making these people highly valuable assets.

However, when it comes to implementing new technologies, it is also important to maintain an open mind and be willing to envision new possibilities, which knowledge of past methods might not predict. This is the out-of-the-box thinking, usually found in greater abundance among the newer, younger staff, which will be needed when implementing some of the potential options opened up by the platform your system will provide.

What is the difference between and expert and an innovator?

An expert knows what cannot be done, ...
while an innovator does not.

Without pushing the bounds, particularly in new technologies, we rarely make large gains or breakthroughs. There will be certain kinds of implementation work that will absolutely require a willingness to embrace a fresh perspective. Do not try to implement new systems simply to do the same processes faster. The new ERP approach, by definition, will eliminate many redundant processing steps. It will take a fresh viewpoint to see the possibilities that will open up.

Therefore, you will see these two distinct types of people on your team, at seemingly opposite poles. This is not a problem since the two can complement each other nicely. Both sets of traits are important for successful implementation of your system, and each will become useful applied to the appropriate tasks. Some tasks will require an abundance of knowledge and careful checking, based on experience. Other tasks require creativity and out of the box thinking. You will need both to accomplish your goals. Once your team can clearly see the path they want to take, and once they fully understand the power of the tools at their disposal, then they will become innovators.

Software, databases, and the hardware they run on, are simply tools. Excellent tools, in well trained and creative hands will produce wonderful results, but for the untrained or unpracticed user, those same tools produce unacceptable output. It takes both skill and imagination to excel with this endeavor, and proper training is a must.

Your team will certainly require assistance from outside service providers that will train staff as needed and help get many of these tasks started. Such training services can be highly focused for each user's specific needs. There is a distinct difference between doing it yourself and going it alone, without taking advantage of training and support services. In fact those kinds of educational services and expert guidance should comprise a significant amount of the non-software budget for the project.

Also previously mentioned as a potential progress constraint, there may well be individuals with a compulsion to keep certain things the same, even though you obviously intend to make serious changes. However as we discussed, there are some instances where you can minimize disruptions by maintaining certain aspects of the "old system", such as the look of documents and other data views. There is no benefit from changing just for the sake of change.

All of these factors can be reconciled through a careful planning process, which starts with the assumption that there is no "standard" solution that will address all of your needs. This is the do it yourself era, and that certainly applies to implementation of your information systems.

Keep in mind that the information system you create becomes the plumbing that connects all of your company's processes. Your vital information is collected through many different methods, from manual input, to bar code scanning, to shop floor data collection, and so on, depending on the circumstances for each process. From there, once that precious data is captured, it is entirely up to your needs how it will be presented to each user in your organization.

Therefore, we have two primary types of components where customization may be needed: data collection (input) and presentation (output). Modern information systems provide tools for the users to customize both types. Whether this work is done entirely by your team or by others, or a combination, is your choice based on the capabilities and availability of time for your people and the contractors you have available.

Here we will look at two types of input:

1. user interfaces for direct, controlled input of a wide range information, and

2. data collection, usually smaller sets of information, often collected dynamically, with an emphasis on low cost/low time.

The best systems for make-to-order manufacturing will also offer user-definable input tools called configurators, which allow input to be controlled and automated on a product by product basis. Each product can have its own set of features and options, with every choice linked to the database. The user can select from a defined list for each feature or option, which also allows the calculations for price and materials required, along with almost anything else you could want.

Many systems also provide a means for user interfaces to be configured; hiding or exposing various elements to users based on each user's permissions and preferences. Some of these options are easy to access and use, while others require significant programming skills. Either way, it is the job of your management team to specify the requirements as early in the process as possible.

Data collection options are abundant and offer a wide range of choices for the many applications found, from your offices, to the warehouse, factory, and even remote and field locations. Particularly with today's LAN's, WAN's, access to Internet connections, and cellular smartphones, there are almost unlimited possibilities for quick and simple data access and collection to meet your requirements.

For all this data to be of any use, you will need methods for selecting, sorting, and presenting it quickly and in a meaningful format. This is an area where modern software tools have really improved, providing some very powerful options, which previously would have required extensive custom programming.

With a well designed relational database as your foundation, there are powerful query tools that can do the selecting and sorting of the data needed for each presentation view. Traditionally that data would then be either printed or presented on screen. A step further is allowing the user to click on data elements, to "drill down" into the underlying data, such as clicking a name reveals more details, or clicking a total brings up the individual items that sum to that number.

Another innovation available in the most flexible systems is the dashboard, as seen in a previous chapter. Dashboards can be designed with multiple views of data, each presented appropriately as needed, in rows and columns, charts and graphs, or in virtually any form supported by your screen. These dashboards can be created for every different user, based on their specific needs, and even multiple dashboards for users with a range of interests. These are really like templates that format the presentation of your data.

For example, the sales manager may want to keep tabs on the number of proposals and their dollar totals, by sales person, or territory. The production manager wants to see the schedule and how the work is progressing, as well as the current workload on each work center in the plant. Purchasing requires a view of the critical materials that need to be ordered, as well as inventories and allocations of key components. The CFO might want to see cash-flow, receivables, payables, and other critical financial perspectives.

The principle value of dashboards is their ability to display many different data elements in one screen presentation. These dashboards can be saved and retrieved, just like custom reports. Unlike reports, with dashboards, multiple kinds of data views can easily be grouped and presented as a collection.

Here again, it is the work of your team to plan and detail the requirements for each of the presentation views you will need. Some are easy to change later, but others will be more costly, so those should be carefully planned from the start.

The possibilities are only limited by your abilities and imagination. Make sure that the system you select provides easy to use tools, which allow your staff to create these valuable data views. Dashboard design and creation should be a standard tool that does not require specialized programming skills.

In a number of our previous examples, we have seen methods of data collection that were integrated into the shop floor processes. Activities that consume materials and other resources can be monitored and allow for multiple transactions to be triggered by simply scanning a bar code indicating a processing stage has been completed.

A single scan or other type of data input, will cause a whole series of material transactions as an assembly passes through a work center. At that same point, other costs were added to the work order, and the assembly was completed through that particular stage in the process. All of this activity will then be instantly visible in the many views we have created, from reports, to dashboards, making your new information system real-time.

Many of these transaction processing activities will be taking place as your system is ramped up for full use. Which brings up one final "do it yourself" issue. Part of the implementation and testing of the system will be to validate the methods and procedures that have been developed as components of your data collection plans. Everything should be verified for accuracy and ease of use.

One of the best ways to know is to do it yourself. Team leaders, shop supervisors, and management, should all play appropriate roles in the testing and validation of these system components. From scanning labels, to complex data entry screens and configurators, all of the steps in the process must be as smooth and simple to use as possible.

Management should carefully validate the new processes themselves before requiring workers to use the system. Doing so will help reduce training costs and errors, as well as improve the overall speed. And one of the most important characteristics we are looking for is data capture that has minimal effect on the process being measured. Make sure that the methods employed do not interfere any more than absolutely necessary with the process they measure.

After each basic setup step, there needs to be careful observation and feedback, with opportunity for fine tuning at that point. This is where the planning and setup work will be put to the test.

Do It Yourself, then Use It Yourself...

One Brick at a Time

No one would try to build the roof of a house before the walls were erected or the foundation laid. But in the world of software, the final result is often expected day one, without any thought to the steps that lead up to those capabilities.

Unless you believe in ancient aliens, the pyramids were an enormous effort, built one stone at a time, from the ground up; certainly not built in a day. The builders had no modern machinery, much less flying saucers with tractor beams to lift the stones. Similarly, there is no shortcut to the top of a complex information system. It cannot be bought or hired out, although with proper planning outside help can certainly reduce the internal workload and help get the job completed more quickly.

Your first priority after the planning stages is loading the data, from the basic elements and on up the levels. This process will probably combine import and cleaning of legacy data, with fresh input from other sources and by manual entry. Once this is underway, you can begin things such as user interface customization, reports, and the many types of data collection that will be needed.

However, as we have seen in many examples, the database is the foundation, so that must be built first and constructed soundly. If this work is done well, then all the applications and customization features will work as required; in fact the data structures must be built with those needs in mind. Getting ahead of the data could require rebuilding subsequent components if anything underneath changes.

The graphic below illustrates the typical building process leading to a fully functional ERP system. The foundation includes the most basic data; materials, people (including CRM), costs, etc. These are the most fundamental building blocks, and if this work is not done well, then everything made from those building blocks will be less reliable. A carefully crafted foundation will support all of the activities your company does to make money. Build it very well.

The second layer of our pyramid is composed of the collections of data, made from the basic elements of cost that comprise the foundation. These collections include BOM's and process routings (collectively called product structures), and other groups of the cost elements that drive your business. Once the collections are built, activities such as, purchasing, production work orders, inventory transactions, and so on, can all begin to take shape.

The next layer in this example, includes more complex activities, such as quoting your products to prospects and customers, leading to sales orders. These components can range from simple order entry for standard products, and go on to include parametric products designed with layers of interdependent features and options.

That parametric category may be driven by product configurators, which for companies that need them, cannot be compromised. These are vital tools for any make-to-order or engineered-to-order type of manufacturing. And as we have explained, the configurator is only practical when connected to a well normalized data structure, which we have just finished setting up.

Finally, once all of these layers are beginning to function, and your careful testing is proving that your data structures are fit to support your business, then the planning tools can be contemplated. This is the "P" in ERP; the pinnacle of our system where management finally goes beyond collecting and presenting results, into the realm of predicting the future. If the supporting levels have been built by our standards of normalization and well implemented to reflect our real world needs and conditions, then we will be in the best position to accurately predict future results.

Much of this category is mostly a matter of purchasing the features, since such planning modules will operate on the data structures that were specifically designed to provide the proper input for this purpose.

These high-level tools can include components such as scheduling (many flavors of this available), capacity planning, and material requirements planning (MRP), all tuned to your specific business needs.

Also at this stage and in many cases a layer or two below, connections outside your facility become possible, such as remote access by members of your team that are in other locations, Web commerce, and any number of other options that current and future technologies allow.

This brick-by-brick building process is governed by more than just the data entry process, but also the scheduling of all the other implementation tasks, because everything is dependent on the data. This is why it makes no sense, for example, to try to jump straight to the estimating module, without already having your costs and product structures in the database and checked. Build everything in layers, in synchronization with input and validation of the data.

Here is an example of some of the types of milestones in a typical implementation process with regard to the database setup and testing procedures:

1. Kick off meeting with all major participants, assign roles, agree on major milestones

2. Prepare hardware and network, install server applications and database

3. Planning for data structures, importing of legacy data, and customization begins

4. Preliminary user training begins, matched to the sequence of module implementation

5. Begin populating database; import clean starting data

6. User data entry begins, filling in lowest levels first

7. Data collections (BOM, routing, and configurators)

8. Begin first use of the system; first Go Live

Certain of these activities can progress independently while others must occur in a specific sequence, requiring foundations to be put down first. Not only must the data go in a level at a time, this is also true of dependencies in many of the processes. Careful planning is necessary to match goals with available resources to meet the schedules. These circumstances are no different than the complex coordination involved in production scheduling in the first place. So in a way the implementation is great practice for basic project management skills which will be valuable well after the system is up and running.

Once you have your data structures well built, and you have begun to utilize the "standard" features of the system, the next wave of the implementation process can begin. This is where the plan becomes special to each company's goals. There will of course, be reports of all kinds, which will be customized to the needs of your business. There will also be many options for the user interface components of the system. These will be must-have features on your system evaluation check list.

Some readers may have noticed that there has been little mention of accounting data or functionality. One reason is that accounting systems are sometimes treated separately from the balance of ERP. Some companies choose to keep their existing system, which hopefully will have reasonably good data connection capabilities, either direct or by import/export. Then there will be others that choose to include accounting modules with the ERP system purchase, which ensures tighter integration, simplifies the need for mapping G/L accounts to and from the ERP, and reduces the need for custom programming.

Either way, as a rule of thumb it is a good idea to limit the scope of activities performed within accounting to the general ledger, receivables & payables, payroll, and related functions. Activities such as purchasing must be completely integrated into the manufacturing process to function in perfect balance with the needs of production flow.

Depending on the types of products your company produces, another significant milestone is designing and building configurators, which are the front-end tools for selecting features and options of a product, generating pricing and a production BOM. If your company does not offer such product options, then a very simple BOM can handle the order processing job.

Sequence of Implementation of Modules by Pyramid Level:

- Level I, Elements: Train users/begin entry and import of; Material, Activities, Machines, overhead values, also begin CRM data import/entry

- Level II, Collections: BOM, Routing, can be combination of import, cleaning, adding data, and manual entry

- Level III, Manufacturing: Work Orders, Purchasing

- Level IV, Sales: Quotations, Sales Orders

- Level V, Planning: Scheduling, Capacity, MRP

These implementation levels are in sequence by the various modules, based on the order that the data elements and structures will be prepared for use. It must be a fairly synchronous process, or time is wasted filling in blanks in cases where information has not yet been input.

Unlike the great pyramids, your information system will never be finished. It will always be a work in progress. However, with a strong foundation, similar to a well constructed building, additions will be easily made.

It is very important to keep this building process in mind right from the beginning. There is no magic wand, even if your company has an excess of cash to invest. No amount of money will allow you to jump to the top of this pyramid.

It must be built brick by brick.

Putting It All Together

Now that the concepts have been presented, with an appropriate amount of a management level perspective on a wide range of subjects. These methods of viewing an ERP environment and the components from which it is constructed provide the principles needed to design your own implementation plan.

We have reached the stage where we must address the biggest challenge; applying the concepts to address our real world objectives. This is the stage where many "how-to" books fall apart, where the reader has reached the end of the book and is still wondering, "so how to I actually apply the these concepts?"

In an effort to avoid a similar fate, this chapter establishes a framework for constructing your own specific plan, applying the principles of simplification and sound data organization that have been presented and validated.

Also keep in mind, purchasing a "complete" ERP package does preclude connections and integration with other software products your company needs for specialize functions. Even the most complete ERP packages on the market will not include highly specialized tools such as, graphics design, engineering CAD systems, or CNC code generation, so these additional tools will often be integrated into your complete system.

From this point, we will assume you have done your homework and selected what you believe to be the best ERP system based on your company's requirements. Your selection will of course meet the following criteria, including:

- a solid database foundation,

- full range of data collection options,

- easily customized presentation of the information,

- connectivity between other networks, hardware, & applications,

- with the flexibility to adapt to constant change

These are basic requirements of your platform. Assuming that you have established that starting point, what kind of implementation process should your team design, now that it is time to get down to the planning process?

What follows is a generic implementation plan, grouped by major milestones that are typical, but your team will edit them with specific details to meet your objectives.

Here are some assumptions:

- Your company will have assistance from either the ERP supplier, or from resources contracted to provide customization, data migration, setup of database and server components, training, and many other support services that will be needed

- From this point forward, for simplicity, we will refer to any supplier or service provider as simply "vendor", which can apply to any software component or service work that is purchased by your company to be delivered by others

- This scenario has some special, but common objectives involving Web-commerce for complex products with many features and options

- All islands will be connected, from sales prospecting through accounting

- Major decisions about data structures have been agreed upon and the overall objectives set

Therefore, given these assumptions, the following is a generic implementation plan. Each milestone is the heading for a collection of activities needed to achieve that stage of completion. In actual practice it is common to use something like Microsoft Project as an organizing and scheduling tool, where all the specific tasks would be detailed.

The level of detail that would comprise the activities and timelines would not be meaningful here, so instead each milestone in this sample describes the general goals and activities in words. Creating a lot of example details at this point would clutter the message, rather than add clarity.

The context of this example plan is entirely from an owner's point of view, not that of an ERP system provider. There will of course be many activities and components of the implementation process that your vendor would provide, however this example is focused primarily on those activities that should be managed internally. Management of these steps should always remain under the system owner's control, even when parts of the project are assigned to outside parties. There will be many tasks throughout your plan that will be assigned to vendor contractors or that will be completed with training and guidance from vendors, all of which will be under the control of (owned by) this project's management team.

Milestone: 1 Launch
At the kick off stage, the primary goals will be to organize resources (internal staff and vendor resources), assigning the required activities

for each objective. The number of people involved in the project may vary as the plan progresses, but there are some essential team members that will remain active throughout the entire project.

At the top, corporate management must take ownership, including involvement in the process at the high level planning stages, as well as routinely monitoring progress. To keep the process at the right pace, it will require VP level participation at a minimum. Each functional group within the organization must have key staff in active participation.

The complete and concise definition of the project objectives will guide the choices with regard to organization of the milestones as well as the skills and experience required for each of the categories of work to be completed.

Typical categories follow the company organization, such as, sales, operations, information systems, engineering, manufacturing, accounting and so on. Each of these functional departments will require a key manager in the most active lead position, with full capabilities of contributing at the decision-making level with regard to their area of responsibility.

The individual in charge of this project will define an organization to address each of the categories of work, assigning individuals or teams to specific tasks in the plan. Throughout the balance of this plan we will see references to the personnel assigned to tasks, which will usually also specify the needed area of expertise, and will often require more than one individual. This scenario will employ members of all of the example categories above — sales through accounting — as the stages of the plan progress.

This launch milestone establishes the timeframe and the defines the organization of the project, which team members will be needed for each subsequent step, and the resources needed. This first milestone would be identical in any implementation plan. The milestones that follow will be vary based on your specific objectives, but our example contains many common tasks.

Milestone: 2 Setup Database Grid

The first tangible implementation step after your plan is defined, is the installation of the components comprising your data grid. This will include the supporting hardware components, followed by installation of software and databases.

Upon completion, you have the hardware installed and configured for your network. Users and permissions will have been setup, based on their activities and authority. Remote access will also be setup for external company users and vendors that will provide services.

SQL Server will be installed on the main file server. Separate machines may be configured for managing other components, including remote access, FTP and Web commerce.

Next is the loading of the first databases, with primarily empty tables at first. At this time the main components of your ERP software will be installed on the server. Client software will be installed on all team members computers, as well as computers for any additional staff assigned to do the first stages of data entry.

A "sandbox" database will also be created at this point for the training and testing activities required throughout this process. This database can be periodically erased if a fresh start is wanted.

The above activities will all be jointly performed by your IT staff and your vendor's technicians. This process is intended, not only to install these components, but also to train your staff to install these modules again at any future date as needed. In this way, your team will gain the experience needed to maintain and expand the system as required to support growth.

This milestone also specifies cleaning and importing certain data from a variety of legacy sources such as:

- your current CRM system (prospects, customers, vendors, employees)

- other databases from operations may provide some starting data for inventory items, routings, and BOM

- establish definitions of the work centers and plant locations, etc., which if previously defined may be imported from the legacy systems

These data preparation and importing activities will be done primarily by your staff with guidance and assistance from the vendor technicians, particularly on methods of importing into the main database. Team members will come from all departments as the initial data structures are setup related to their areas. All testing will be first be done in the sandbox database until the records are certified by the team leader.

In preparation for your trial run milestone, this testing plan includes several products that will be processed from quotation through all stages for manufacturing, shipment, and invoicing. To achieve this goal, you will need all the supporting data cleaned and setup with all required attributes prior to the trial run. A trial run data setup is one of the requirements for completion of this milestone.

Milestone: 3 Configuration Templates
This milestone will consist of two phases: a trial and a rollout. The trial phase will include only the selected products needed for the system trail run, and these products will be used to validate the architecture of your configurator design, as well as proving out the price calculations.

Other than initial training, these activities will be performed by a team from engineering and sales (for layout design issues and the costing input). The basic functionality will already have been modeled in spreadsheets that sales has developed for pricing simulation. Your team will incorporate that logic into the trial configurators, and connect the data to the sandbox database for the first phase of testing.

The screen layouts of the internal version will be designed by your sales department, taking into account the list of features and screen design tools you will now be able to employ for controlling the order entry and validation process. The engineering members of your team will have already been trained in the specifics of the configurator component, which is really a spreadsheet that acts as the template to manage the selection of features and options.

Your configurators can also address any number of needed restrictions on user entry choices that experience has shown to have been the cause of errors with your current process. These controls will reduce the chances for configurations that are not within the scope of the product design.

The first group of configurators on your schedule will be for the products in the trail run. During the building of these, your team will have assistance from your vendor technicians in the form of training and help with any design or data connection issues that arise.

Once this first cycle is completed, your team will have the knowledge and experience to design and build the rest of the configurators on their own. That process will continue, with a final target of completion by the Go Live milestone.

Milestone : 4 Interface & Reports

Your new ERP system provides tools for a great deal of customization of the user interface as well as reports. All departments are affected and will have participated in drafting the specifications for most of these components.

Members from each department will have submitted:

- mock-ups of each needed report, complete with references to the sources for each data element

- descriptions of user-defined data elements and other modifications to the interface components

- descriptions and layouts of the dashboards needed for the initial Go Live configuration

Two members of your team will have taken the training on the report designer software, and with some additional training from your vendor, they will do a substantial number of the reports. There may be a few exceptions that appear too complex, which can be sub-contracted to your vendor. They will also help your team by answering their questions on difficult reports.

The vendor will have separately quoted the customizations needed for the production and inventory interfaces. These will be delivered prior to the Go Live milestone.

Two members of your team will have completed training to build your own dashboards. One of your engineering staff and one from operations will be working on these for each of the departments, all based on the input they receive. Since you may have never had anything like this, dashboards will be a work in progress, changing as your managers needs change. For this reason, your own staff should learn to build and maintain them.

The team leader must coordinate to ensure all of the specifications and other needed input are submitted in accordance with your schedule. There is a lot of work that will be taken on internally, therefore your time must be managed carefully.

Milestone: 5 Trial Run; Quotation to Invoice

This phase of your implementation will test your data and processes from quotation all the way through invoicing. As a result, team members from every functional area will be involved in this test. The plan is to process several quotations for different assortments of products, each configured with unique features and options.

The initial quotations will utilize your first product configurators, which will incorporate many of the solutions which have been developed through your planning process. Your testing therefore needs to push all the new buttons, in many combinations, to verify your design and the calculations that drive the orders. Sales and engineering team members will have coordinated to develop the scenarios that will test the configurations with as many of the features and options as needed to provide confidence the data works correctly, generating correct results.

Sales orders will then be generated by converting directly from the quotations, eliminating the manual entry necessary with the current system. At that point the team will modify a few orders to test making additional changes to the attributes of some of the products. Sales team members will do all of this phase of the testing.

Once they have completed the sales order processing phase, the next step will be to convert the sales orders to manufacturing work orders. Engineering team members will then check the products and their structures to ensure the BOM and processing activities are all consistent with your defined benchmarks.

At that point the work orders will be scheduled and released, generating demand for materials. This is the point where your team members from operations (production planning, purchasing, and inventory control) will join the test. That group will exercise the components needed for the manufacturing activities that follow.

The entire materials cycle will then be tested, starting with purchasing against the created demand, including a few RFQ tests. Once PO's are in the system, the receiving testing will begin by validating the scanning of incoming material into inventory. There will also be some introduction of shortages and defective materials, to test those features.

Materials will be moved from inventory into WIP by processing both back flushing and manual input, depending on the inventory class for each item in the BOM. Reporting on these transactions will be validated carefully.

Next your team will complete the work order, putting the finished items into finished goods inventory and reviewing the accumulated costs. The sales order will then be ready for shipment, which will be scheduled for the next truck.

Shipping will scan each product as it is loaded on the truck. Then those scans will be verified against the products on the original order. Upon confirmation that the correct items have been loaded on the truck, the packing list will be printed and the order will be set up for invoicing by accounting.

These steps complete the sequence of events that this test will include. Once completed, all the related reports and other views will be checked by members of each department against their benchmark calculations. They will also perform checking for omissions which are the most difficult errors to spot. Use the benchmark data as a checklist to help verify that every transaction has been recorded.

Results from the testing and reports will be reviewed by the entire team. Positive results allow the process to move to the next milestone. Otherwise, depending on the nature of the problems, rework will cause delay.

Putting It All Together

This is also the point at which we you will move off the sandbox database for all but testing and training exercises. Once your team is confident with the quality of your data and your processes, they will switch users over to the main database in preparation for the Go Live milestone.

Milestone: 6 Final Customizations

Upon passing the test phase, you will also have had a chance to work with each of the interface components, reports, and the configurators. That experience provides your team with the opportunity to make adjustments in any of those that would improve their usefulness. Careful notes and commentary about these elements will be very useful once they reach this stage where the fine tuning can be done.

This milestone also marks the deadline for customizations that are in your plan but have not yet been completed. Mostly reports will fall into this last category, but there may be other interface modifications and certainly dashboards that were non-critical to the trial stage.

Milestone: 7 Green Light

Having run the prior gauntlet, you are at the last review point in the process. A great deal of experience will have been gained along the way. Now is the time to make any additional course corrections that were found to be necessary in the testing and training phases to this point.

Your team will have been working with the real database, preparing everything for the Go Live milestone. Verification of the completeness of the data structures and accuracy of the entries will have been done by each department.

Client software will have been installed for all users, including those who were not members of the implementation team. Training on all software and basic procedures will have been completed.

Links have also been completed that connect the engineering department's CAD, CNC code generation, and other specialized software to your materials and work order tables. This work will probably been contracted out to your vendor, since they have experience from other customers that use similar engineering software, and they know the inner workings of the databases.

An audit of the test transaction data will have been completed. The results of the audit will have been presented during the last meeting, for review and approval by top management. This represents "sign-off" through this level of testing. You have a green light to proceed.

Procedures have been finalized and all users have been through basic level training on the new processing methods. Each department manager will now develop plans to ensure the teams have been adequately prepared by the training and running pilot testing of their processes.

Milestone: 8 Go Live
This phase begins with clearing out any test data and will ensure that the database is at a clean starting point. Next your team will do a combination of importing and manual entry to add in those transactions which establish your Go Live starting point.

Fresh starting balances will be setup, based on the physical inventory taken to validate your starting point for accounting. Team members from operations and accounting will complete these tasks.

With all processes running, data validation will continue for several weeks, with department managers and the team leader meeting weekly to review the results.

Milestone: 9 Accounting Connections
Once your team has carefully validated the quality of your transaction data for several weeks, and the review meetings confirm that it all

looks good, then you can make the final connections that will post transactions to accounting.

These will include invoice processing after shipment, inventory transactions, accounts payables triggered by receipts, and other cost related events. This integration is expected to substantially reduce the current workload caused by the huge amount of manual entry needed for these kinds of transactions.

Employees will begin time tracking, picked up through work order transactions on the shop floor, as well as other types of direct and indirect labor cost collection. These transactions will be validated by accounting and then passed to your payroll processor for payment.

Material transactions will also be posted as a result of the shop floor data collection systems now in place. Accounting will be connected for payables from the point of incoming inspection in the receiving department. In a similar manner, truck loading and printing of a packing list will trigger transactions to accounts receivable. Accounting team members along with a few people from operations, will test these connections and verify the correctness of the postings.

These integrations and the improvements in the systems on the manufacturing side of your business will finally relieve your accounting department of the enormous amount of manual transaction volume that has been burdening them for so long. As a result, you can expect financial reporting will now be more timely and accurate.

Milestone: 10 MRP, Planning, CRM

With all of the layers in your pyramid built and tested, your team is at the pinnacle, ready for the final brass ring at the top. The excellent quality of timely transaction data flowing through your grid, provides a wealth of valuable management information; the icing on your cake.

Rescheduling orders, which has been a very manual and risky process, will be easier, faster, and much more reliable, since it will all be connected to the materials and other needed resources.

MRP will make the purchasing department much more proactive, and capable of combining and timing shipments for lower costs and better synchronization with your production schedule. And since you may also make some components to stock, the MRP will help production staff plan work orders for those items as well.

Your CRM tools will have been implemented along the testing process, starting with the first order processing. Therefore, now that your system is in full swing, these tools will help at every step throughout the sales cycle and bring your sales staff up to the state of the art in terms of marketing capabilities. With the drudgery of the configuration and quotation process removed, sales staff will have substantially more time to nurture new business opportunities and build relationships.

Although this completes your implementation, it also lays the groundwork for a Phase II. The configurators that were built will now be the templates for your new Web commerce component on your expanded and upgraded Website.

To summarize, the above example implementation plan builds a solid and reliable data management infrastructure, using a step-by-step building process. With these general milestones as a starting point, and incorporating all of your own specifications, it becomes a simple matter of taking the time to carefully design a specific plan, perfectly tuned to the exact needs of your business.

Rewards of a Healthy Database

So what are the benefits after all the time, effort, investment?

Is ERP really worth the risky, costly, difficult process?

Here are some answers, in one more bullet-pointed list:

- Solid reliable data grid, supporting all business processes, safely backed up and protected, ready for any future expansion in capacity

- Islands replaced by integration between ERP database structures and our other important applications like engineering CAD systems and the production data that controls CNC machining centers

- Your platform is the most up to date, and you can easily maintain it, keeping current with advances in the underlying technology as well as improvements to the application and new modules

- Because of the standards this system provides, connectivity through almost any available technology is possible; from bar coding, to apps on smartphones

- Your Web commerce portal is connected through configurators, real-time to your database, with automation and ease-of-use features that rival or exceed your biggest and best competitors

- The sales process with CRM manages the entire cycle from prospecting, to proposals, through order processing, then tying it all together with the related documents and correspondence

- Every process that generates money transactions is now fully integrated through accounting, eliminating huge amounts of manual entry time and errors, and also allowing for more timely financial reporting

- Production management can view the future, spotting bottlenecks while there is still time to correct the course. This applies to both material and capacity constraints, and schedule changes can be as simple as drag and drop

- All of the planning capability will also allow you to substantially reduce inventory, freeing up cash

- Labor costs, processing time, and errors are all reduced, generating more profit

- These efficiencies allow your company to take on more business

Index

5
5-S, 100, 104

6
6-Sigma, 100

B
back flushing, 51, 154
bar code, 74, 114, 147, 154, 165, 186
BOM
    definition, 109
    flat, 128
    multi level, 129, 130
    pre-defined levels, 131, 133
bottlenecks, 17, 45, 55, 163
building consensus, 10, 98, 177

C
configuration, 111
configurator, 77, 113, 117, 153
continuous improvement, 33, 100
cost accounting, 20, 21, 62
CRM, 85

D
database normalization
    definition, 101
    main topic, 119–144
    results, 124, 139
data collection, 90, 107, 118, 154, 161, 164, 170, 183, 188
data structures
    flat files, 120
    relational, 122

E
ERP definition, 1–3

F
flow charting, 101

I
implementation plan, 90, 99
    example plan, 194–207
integration of processes, 22
intelligent numbers, 29–32
inventory
    balances, 27–29, 47–54
    reduction, 60, 69

J

JIT, 45

K

Kaizen, 100

Kanban, 52

L

labor categories, 26, 159, 165, 206

lean concepts, 24, 40, 89, 100, 126, 148, 162

legacy systems, 5, 24, 123, 130, 136, 143, 147

logic and proof, 35

M

measurements, 4, 9, 17, 20, 21, 25, 38, 56, 155, 164, 169, 187

MRP, 28, 30, 44

O

Object Oriented Programming, 146–151

P

parametric, 87, 112, 127, 190

production scheduling, 72, 82, 116

product structure

    components of, 125

    definition, 109

    graphical illustration, 138

R

return on investment, 22, 37

routing, 74, 107, 125, 127, 138

S

serial and lot tracking, 115

server

    cloud, 96

    hosted, 96

simplification, 100–118

SQL queries, 123–124

staging, 28

stored procedure, 124

synchronization, 92

Synergy

    definition, 13

    examples, 75, 84, 109, 166

T

tablet computer, 156

template, 113, 115

Theory of Constraints, 100

throughput, 7, 26, 40, 49, 55, 91, 107, 163, 165

touch screen, 156

tracking, 72, 114, 166

traveler, 166–167

trigger, 123

V

value, 37

W

Web commerce, 76, 113

work center, 43, 61, 69, 107, 114, 154, 165, 169

work order, 114, 116, 135, 154, 155, 165, 186, 189

CPSIA information can be obtained
at www.ICGtesting.com
Printed in the USA
BVHW061525250322
632218BV00002B/155